PRAYERS
that UNLOCK
FAVOR

PRAYERS that UNLOCK FAVOR

JOHN ECKHARDT

CHARISMA HOUSE

While the author has made every effort to provide accurate, up-to-date source information at the time of publication, statistics and other data are constantly updated. Neither the publisher nor the author assumes any responsibility for errors or for changes that occur after publication. Further, the publisher and author do not have any control over and do not assume any responsibility for third-party websites or their content.

For more resources like this, visit charismahouse.com and the author's website at impactnetwork.global.

Cataloging-in-Publication Data is on file with the Library of Congress.
International Standard Book Number: 978-1-63641-335-8
E-book ISBN: 978-1-63641-336-5

23 24 25 26 27 — 987654321
Printed in the United States of America

Most Charisma Media products are available at special quantity discounts for bulk purchase for sales promotions, premiums, fund-raising, and educational needs. For details, call us at (407) 333-0600 or visit our website at www.charismamedia.com.

CONTENTS

INTRODUCTION

Thou hast granted me life and favour, and thy
visitation hath preserved my spirit.

—JOB 10:12, KJV

THERE IS NOTHING like the favor of God. God's favor
opens doors that no man can shut and shuts doors
no man can open. It brings prosperity and breakthroughs
and makes things easy for you that are difficult for others.

Favor means "grace"; "that which affords joy, pleasure,
delight, sweetness, charm, loveliness" and "goodwill, ben-
efit, bounty, reward." If you look up the Hebrew and Greek
definitions of *prosperity*, many of these words carry over
into favor as well.

Favor is goodwill, God's loving-kindness and benev-
olence given to those who love Him. Favor will release
great blessings, including prosperity, health, opportunity,
and advancement. The Bible records numerous examples
of God's favor upon His people causing them to experience many breakthroughs.

Joseph experienced God's favor and went from prison
to the palace. Although the journey took time, the hand of

God on Jacob's life was unmistakable and brought blessing and abundance to everything he undertook. God will do the same for you. He can radically change your circumstances in one day no matter where you are in life. This is what happens when you're walking in the favor of God.

Esther also operated in the favor of God. She "obtained favor in the sight of all who saw her," and "the king loved Esther more than any other woman because she had gained grace and favor in his sight more than all the virgins. So he set the royal crown on her head and made her queen instead of Vashti" (Est. 2:15, 17). She became queen, even though the kingdom was full of beautiful women who wanted to marry the king, all because she had the favor of God on her life.

God's favor on King Solomon caused him to rise to unparalleled levels of greatness and prosperity. Like Joseph and Esther, he had what I call the favor advantage. Because of the favor of God on his life, Solomon became the wealthiest and greatest king of his day.

We don't need luck. We need the favor of God. When you have God's favor and blessing, nothing in life can hold you down. And when the favor of the Lord is on your life, others will recognize it.

The favor of God on your life is one of the most powerful things that can be released to you. Matthew 6:33 says, "Seek ye first the kingdom of God, and his righteousness;

and *all* these things shall be added unto you" (KJV, emphasis added). God says, "You don't need money. You need My favor." You need His shalom—the full measure of peace—to operate in your life.

This is His gift to you if you are in covenant with Him as His child. God blesses His people and rescues them. Just as He did with the Israelites, God loved you and chose you despite who you are and what you have done. You are elected by God. You were chosen before the foundation of the world. He chose you. It wasn't because of anything you'd done. That is His favor!

In Ezekiel 16:1–14 God talks to the children of Israel about how He found them in a rejected state where they had been thrown away and no one wanted them. They were drowning in their own blood. But when God passed by them, He said to them, "Live!" Then He blessed them and adorned them with jewels. God is saying this same thing to you. Maybe you were thrown away to die and had no chance at living. Maybe no one wanted you or you were not born with a silver spoon in your mouth. But when God looked upon you, He had mercy on you.

God will not only save you and wash you, but He will also bless you, dress you up, put jewels on you, and beautify you. The grace and favor of God on your life will cause you to go into a place of prosperity. God will not only save you but also multiply you and bless you. I've seen Him do this in my own life.

THE POWER OF FAVOR

Growing up in Chicago, I spent most of my early life in one small block of the city until I got married. My mother—a full-blooded Sicilian—was a devout Catholic, and of course she wanted me to go to Catholic school. As a single parent, money was tight, but somehow she scraped together enough to send me to Holy Angels Catholic School. I went to Catholic school from kindergarten to eighth grade, when a Catholic priest suddenly blessed my life. He came to me and said I had been chosen to go to a private high school in the suburbs.

The priest told me that a sponsor had come forward and offered to pay my tuition for all four years at Loyola Academy, a private, all-boys school at the time and one of the top schools in the city. I was going to school with the "rich kids." I had to ride the train every day from my small block in the middle of Chicago to the suburb of Wilmette, Illinois, with kids who lived in neighborhoods entirely different from mine.

I'll never forget: my sponsor was the owner of a large company, and I had the chance to spend time in his home. I'm from a little apartment in Chicago, and there I was staying with this man and his family in their mansion. This is the favor of God.

In my senior year at Loyola Academy, some faculty members came and asked me where I wanted to go to college. I said, "Well, I think I want to go to Northwestern." I didn't realize it was one of the most expensive schools in the Big 10. They said, "OK, we're going to give you a scholarship and pay your way to go to Northwestern." I was going to school with people who had money, and I didn't have enough sense to know I wasn't "supposed" to fit in. I didn't have enough sense to be intimidated or think I didn't belong. I had the favor of God on my life and didn't know it.

In my junior year at Northwestern I got saved and began attending Crusaders Church. Now with salvation the blessing of God really came. When I got saved, I gave my whole heart to God. I plunged into this thing. I was all the way in. I told all my friends goodbye. They thought I was crazy. I wouldn't get high with them anymore. I wouldn't drop acid anymore. I gave all that up when I got saved in 1978.

I was the first one in my family, among my friends, and in my neighborhood to be saved, and it wasn't because of me. I didn't have enough sense to get saved. Sin makes you a fool. It was the favor of God that called me out of where I was and drew me in.

Since that time the favor of God has increased in my life.

God has taken me around the world. I have ministered in seventy nations. I've met prime ministers and presidents. I've been to the White House. None of this was because of me. I am a man who grew up in the hood. So I'm not just talking about something I read in the Bible. I'm telling you, when the favor of God comes on your life, it will take you places you could not go on your own. You might not have a dime in your pocket, but God says, "Don't worry. You don't need money; you need favor. I'll have somebody pay for it for you."

IN THE FAVOR OF GOD IS LIFE

It is such a blessing to be granted favor! Other definitions of favor include "preferential treatment," "to be partial to," "to make easier," "to support," "to perform a kindness for," "favoritism; goodwill; liking." Synonyms for favor include prefer, like, approve, endorse, support, lean toward, honor, be partial to, grant favors to, further, promote, treat with partiality, show consideration for, make an exception for, use one's influence for, treat as a special character.

This is what God will do for you. You can live with divine assistance and intervention. You can enjoy "favored child" status and enjoy the blessing of God's favor.

I see people all the time who aren't enjoying life. Their lives are full of pain and difficulty, and my heart breaks for them. I don't believe God wants His people to live in misery. We all face challenges in life, but I don't believe God intended for His people to be unhappy, full of worry, and always troubled with family and marital problems, financial issues, and poor health.

Proverbs 8:35 says, "For whoso findeth me findeth life, and shall obtain favour of the LORD" (KJV). And Psalm 30:5 says, "In His favor is life." Jesus came that we might have life and have it more abundantly (John 10:10). In the favor of God is life. God says, "When you get My favor, you get life."

Several translations of Psalm 30:5—including the AMP, ESV, and NASB—say, "His favor is for a lifetime." God intends for you to live your entire life with His favor. God wants to give you favor all the days of your life—not just for a few months or years. You can be happy and satisfied enjoying the blessings of God throughout your lifetime. But you must live a lifestyle that God favors.

God favors certain things. God doesn't favor sin, rebellion, witchcraft, or perversion, for instance. He doesn't favor pride, wickedness, lying, or deceit. To walk in the favor of God, you must live a lifestyle that attracts God's favor.

In this book, we will look at nine keys that unlock the favor of God: righteousness, wisdom, humility, generosity, knowledge, mercy and truth, excellence, and prayer. Some Christians think God's favor is random, that He favors some and not others for no reason. But God is not a random god. We don't have to hope that maybe God will bless us. We can live in such a way that our very lives unlock the favor of God.

As we study these keys, we are also going to learn declarations and prayers based on God's Word that will activate His favor and shalom. Proverbs 18:21 states, "Death and life are in the power of the tongue." We can choose blessing by choosing to live and speak correctly.

I believe there's going to be a revival of favor in your life. If you feel like you have no favor, get ready for some favor to come. Sometimes all we have to do is make a minor adjustment for things to begin to happen and flow in our lives.

God is ready to release new favor, blessing, prosperity, protection, and peace over you. It is His desire to give you good things. Now get ready to receive them.

CHAPTER 1

RIGHTEOUSNESS—THE FOUNDATION OF FAVOR

For thou, LORD, wilt bless the righteous; with favour
wilt thou compass him as with a shield.

—PSALM 5:12, KJV

RIGHTEOUSNESS IS A subject many believers don't
fully understand. But if you want to walk in the favor
of God, you must get a revelation that if you are saved, you
are the righteousness of God in Christ.

For he hath made him to be sin for us, who knew
no sin; that we might be made the righteousness
of God in him.

—2 CORINTHIANS 5:21, KJV

Jesus was made to be sin so that you could be made the
righteousness of God in Him. This is an exchange. Jesus
became sin; you become righteous.

…that God was in Christ reconciling the world to
Himself, not counting people's sins against them
[but canceling them]. And He has committed to

us the message of reconciliation [that is, restoration to favor with God].

—2 Corinthians 5:19, amp

Jesus died that we might be reconciled with God. *Reconcile* means "to restore to friendship or harmony."[1] Reconciliation puts us back in right standing with God, which is the definition of righteousness. Reconciliation restores us to favor with God. Our repentance followed by Christ's forgiveness starts the process.

Blessed and happy and favored are those whose lawless acts have been forgiven, and whose sins have been covered up and completely buried. Blessed and happy and favored is the man whose sin the Lord will not take into account nor charge against him.

—Romans 4:7–8, amp

This is the foundation of favor: we repent, Jesus brings forgiveness, we accept it, our sins are forgiven, and we are back in favor with God. The forgiven believer is the blessed and favored believer.

Favor comes to those whose sins are forgiven. So if you have repented, God has forgiven your sins, and He remembers them no more. You are now in favored status.

So then those who are people of faith [whether Jew or Gentile] are blessed and favored by God

[and declared free of the guilt of sin and its pen-
alty, and placed in right standing with Him]
along with Abraham, the believer.

—GALATIANS 3:9, AMP

Forgiveness and righteousness are received by faith.
This faith begins to release the favor of God into our lives.
Free from guilt, shame, and condemnation, we can now
enjoy, confess, and walk in the favor of God, which is
available to us by faith.

ACCESS GOD'S PROMISES BY FAITH

There are great blessings, benefits, and promises that come
to us as children of God, and we access them by faith. If
you are not enjoying the fullness you have in Christ, your
faith may need to be enlarged. I believe that by faith you
can inherit the promises, rest, joy, peace, favor, glory, and
all the great things that belong to us children of God. It is
a spiritual inheritance.

God wants you to enjoy His blessings and promises that
are in Christ. The more revelation and understanding you
receive, the more you can confess this and believe and
walk in this. Whatever your current situation, faith will
turn your whole life around. Faith will cause you to move
out of a place of poverty, lack, strife, heaviness, fear, and
stress and into a place of victory, abundance, joy, shalom,

favor, and all the promises of God that are in Christ, yes and amen, meaning "it is so."

Don't let any church, denomination, doctrine, believer, unbeliever, or family member keep you out of the fullness of what Christ has for you. Begin to confess and believe His promises, appropriating them by faith. That means you declare the promises, stand on the promises, and fight hell with the promises.

The enemy will work overtime on your mind and emotions to keep you in an exhausted and frustrated state so you will believe God's favor is for super saints and not you. This is a lie. Like many people with mega potential, there may be times when you feel stuck outside of your promises because you have unconsciously partnered with the lies of hell. This is one of Satan's strategies to get you to believe his lies, make vows and partner with him, and empower demon spirits to wreak havoc in your life.

How does this happen? You hear words such as, "Things will never work out for you," and then begin to agree with the deception and speak it over yourself: "Things will never work out for me." This is the work of the enemy, and as he influences what you speak, his demons will honor your word. They understand the realm of covenant and keep you on the outskirts of God's best for you by sowing lies into your heart and mind.

You must rise up, break those lies, renew your mind,

and begin to prophesy the blessings and favor of God. God's favor is not just for others; it is for you! As a child of God you are loved, protected, and provided for. You have been stuck and depleted long enough. The enemy has sapped and drained you for far too long, but heaven has resources for every area of your life.

Refuse to accept anything less than the promises of God. You have been made righteous in Christ Jesus and all the promises of God are yes in Him and amen. Rise up in faith and believe in the goodness of God. Decree that you will live in the favor of God. Stand on the Word of the Lord and move into the place of peace, promise, favor, and reward.

Use the prayers and declarations in this chapter to confess your righteousness in Christ and let faith arise so you can lay hold of what is yours.

PRAYERS OF THE RIGHTEOUS

Lord, do not allow my soul to famish, and do not cast away my desire (Prov. 10:3).

Lord, I cast my burden on You, and You will sustain me. You will not permit me to be moved (Ps. 55:22).

Lord, You have discerned that I am righteous and one who serves You. Make me Your jewel (Mal. 3:17–18).

Lord, let me be counted worthy of Your kingdom (2 Thess. 1:5).

Lord, bring my soul out of prison that I may praise Your name. Let the righteous surround me, for You will deal bountifully with me (Ps. 142:7).

Lord, let it be granted to me to be arrayed in fine linen, clean and bright (Rev. 19:8).

Lord, let the righteous requirement of the law be fulfilled in me (Rom. 8:4).

"Oh, let the wickedness of the wicked come to an end, but establish the just; for the righteous God tests the hearts and minds" (Ps. 7:9, NKJV).

Far be it from You, O Lord, to slay the righteous with the wicked. You, the Judge of all the earth, will do right (Gen. 18:25).

Hear in heaven, O Lord, and act, and judge Your servants, condemning the wicked, bringing his way on his head. Justify the righteous according to his righteousness (1 Kings 8:32).

I thank You, Lord, for the crown of righteousness that is laid up for me, for You will give it to me on that day—and not just to me, but to all who have loved Your appearing (2 Tim. 4:8).

"Hear me when I call, O God of my righteousness" (Ps. 4:1).

"God is with the generation of the righteous." My enemies are in great fear (Ps. 14:5).

Because I practice righteousness, I am righteous, just as He is righteous (1 John 3:7).

Let the Lord reward me according to my righteousness, and according to the cleanliness of my hands may He reward me (2 Sam. 22:21).

Let me not trust in my own righteousness, despising others (Luke 18:9).

I hunger and thirst for righteousness. Lord, fill me (Matt. 5:6).

Lord, let me walk in the way of goodness and keep to the paths of righteousness (Prov. 2:20, NKJV).

Let me not find treasures in wickedness, which profits me nothing, but let righteousness deliver me from death (Prov. 10:2).

Let blessings be upon my head (Prov. 10:6).

Let righteousness guard my way so that I will be found blameless (Prov. 13:6).

Let me be repaid with good (Prov. 13:21).

Let me not be reproached by sin but exalted in righteousness (Prov. 14:34).

Let not my ways be an abomination unto the Lord (Prov. 15:9).

Lord, do not be far from me. Hear my prayer (Prov. 15:29).

The eyes of the Lord are on me, and His ears are open to my cry (Ps. 34:15).

Many are my afflictions, but Lord, You deliver me out of them all (Ps. 34:19).

Let light and gladness be sown for me (Ps. 97:11, KJV).

Prayers and Declarations to Increase Faith

I declare that I have uncommon, great faith in the power of Jesus Christ; faith that cannot be found anywhere else (Matt. 8:10).

Let it be to me according to my faith (Matt. 9:29).

I activate my mustard seed of faith and say to this mountain of sickness and disease in my life, "Be removed and go to another place." Nothing will be impossible for me (Matt. 17:20).

I have faith in God (Mark 11:22).

I go in peace because my faith has saved me (Luke 7:50).

I pray as Your anointed disciples prayed, "Increase my faith!" (Luke 17:5).

My faith will not fail (Luke 22:32).

Like Stephen, I do great wonders and signs because I am full of faith (Acts 6:8).

"The just shall live by faith" (Rom. 1:17).

The righteousness of God is revealed to me through faith in Jesus (Rom. 3:22).

I am justified by my faith in Jesus (Rom. 3:26).

By faith the promises of God are sure to me, the seed of Abraham (Rom. 4:16).

I will not stagger at the promises of God through unbelief, but I will stand strong in the faith, giving glory to God (Rom. 4:20, KJV).

I have access by faith to the grace of God (Rom. 5:2).

My faith increases the more I hear, and I hear by the Word of God (Rom. 10:17).

My faith is "not in the wisdom of men but in the power of God" (1 Cor. 2:5).

The Spirit of God has given me the gift of faith (1 Cor. 12:9).

I am established and anointed by God (2 Cor. 1:21).

No man has dominion over my faith. I stand by faith (2 Cor. 1:24).

I walk by faith and not by sight (2 Cor. 5:7).

I am a child of Abraham because I have faith (Gal. 3:7).

By faith I receive the promises of God in my life (Gal. 3:22).

I am a child of God because I have faith in Christ Jesus (Gal. 3:26).

Because of my faith in Jesus I have boldness and confident access to approach God (Eph. 3:12).

I take the shield of faith and quench all the fiery darts of the wicked one (Eph. 6:16).

I am raised to life through faith in Christ (Col. 2:12).

I put "on the breastplate of faith and love" (1 Thess. 5:8).

I will not suffer shipwreck in my life because I have "faith and a good conscience" (1 Tim. 1:19).

I obtain for myself "good standing and great boldness" in my faith in Christ Jesus (1 Tim. 3:13).

I will not be sluggish. I will "imitate those who through faith and patience inherit the promises" of God (Heb. 6:12, NKJV).

I declare that I feel the substance and see the evidence of the things for which I have faith (Heb. 11:1).

I see through the eyes of faith the promise of things afar off. I am persuaded of their reality. I embrace them, knowing that I am a stranger and pilgrim on this earth (Heb. 11:13).

I will forsake any bondage that seeks to entrap me, looking forward by faith and setting my eyes on Him who is invisible (Heb. 11:27).

I decree and declare that by faith I will walk through my trials on dry ground, and my enemies will drown (Heb. 11:29).

I will encircle the immovable walls in my life, and by my faith those walls will fall down (Heb. 11:30).

I will subdue kingdoms, administer justice, obtain promises, and stop the mouths of lions because of my faith (Heb. 11:33).

I will stand firm and not waver. I will come boldly before God, asking in faith (Jas. 1:6).

My faith is alive (Jas. 2:17).

I will show my faith by the works I do (Jas. 2:18).

I declare that my faith works together with my works, and by my works my faith is made perfect (Jas. 2:22).

My faith and hope are in God (1 Pet. 1:21).

CHAPTER 2

WISDOM-FAVOR'S MASTER KEY

For whoever finds me [wisdom] finds life, and will
obtain favor of the LORD.

—PROVERBS 8:35

RIGHTEOUSNESS IS THE foundation of favor, but wisdom is the master key that unlocks it.

There is no substitute for wisdom. If you were to ask, "What is the most important thing for a successful life?" very few would answer, "Wisdom." But Proverbs 4:7 tells us that wisdom is the principal or primary thing you will need for success in life.

Whoever finds wisdom finds life and obtains favor from the Lord (Prov. 8:35). Wisdom includes prudence, discretion, knowledge, understanding, counsel, subtlety, and discernment. We need these things if we want to live a life of favor.

The Bible says a wise servant has the favor of the King.

The king's favour is toward a wise servant: but his
wrath is against him that causeth shame.

—PROVERBS 14:35, KJV

> Who then is a faithful and wise servant, whom
> his lord hath made ruler over his household, to
> give them meat in due season?
>
> —MATTHEW 24:45, KJV

Are you a wise servant of the King? Do you steward the gifts God has given you with wisdom? Is wisdom a part of your life and decisions? This is a key to walking in the favor of God.

Solomon was the wisest of kings, and he received great favor from the Lord.

> And the speech pleased the LORD, that Solomon
> had asked this thing. And God said unto him,
> Because thou hast asked this thing, and hast not
> asked for thyself long life; neither hast asked riches
> for thyself, nor hast asked the life of thine ene-
> mies; but hast asked for thyself understanding to
> discern judgment; Behold, I have done according
> to thy words: lo, I have given thee a wise and an
> understanding heart; so that there was none like
> thee before thee, neither after thee shall any arise
> like unto thee.
>
> —1 KINGS 3:10–12, KJV

Solomon was not only given wisdom, but God "magni-fied him exceedingly" (2 Chron. 1:1, KJV). As a result of God's favor on his life, Solomon had favor with kings and queens. King "Hiram gave Solomon cedar trees and fir trees according to all his desire" (1 Kings 5:10, KJV). The queen of Sheba came to hear the wisdom of Solomon and brought a train of costly gifts to him (1 Kings 10:2). This is the power of God's favor.

Solomon became the wealthiest and greatest king of his day (1 Kings 10:10, 25). He was the most blessed man of his generation and was exalted and promoted because of God's favor. God made Solomon famous.

Sadly, Solomon lost this favor later in his life because he married strange women and worshipped strange gods. Pride gripped his heart, and he lost the favor that made him great. His kingdom was split after his death because of his disobedience.

WISDOM AND THE FEAR OF GOD

"The fear of the LORD is the beginning of wisdom, and the knowledge of the Holy One is understanding" (Prov. 9:10). The fear of the Lord is the beginning of wisdom; therefore, the fear of the Lord is connected to favor.

> Praise the LORD! (Hallelujah!) Blessed [fortunate, prosperous, and favored by God] is the man who fears the LORD [with awe-inspired reverence and worships Him with obedience], who delights greatly in His commandments.
>
> —PSALM 112:1, AMP

The blessed, prosperous, and favored man is the man that fears the Lord with awe-inspired reverence.

> Blessed [happy and sheltered by God's favor] is everyone who fears the Lᴏʀᴅ [and worships Him with obedience], who walks in His ways and lives according to His commandments.
>
> —Psalm 128:1, AMP

Listening with reverence and awe (fear) to the voice of God over your life and then walking in obedience to what you hear is wisdom. God will not steer you wrong. He has set the boundary lines—His path for you to have abundant life and great favor—out before you. He has set you in a pleasant place (Ps. 16:6). He leads you by still and quiet (peaceful) waters and restores your soul (Ps. 23:2–3). To fear God means that you are careful to follow His guidance and direction, knowing that you risk your very life if you don't. (See Matthew 10:28.) When you fear God, you are submitted to His ways and trust that He has a good plan for your life (Jer. 29:11).

A Crown of Favor

Proverbs 4:9 tells us that wisdom will deliver to us a crown of favor: "She [Wisdom] shall give to thine head an ornament of grace: a crown of glory shall she deliver to thee" (ᴋᴊᴠ). A crown is an ornament. An ornament is a thing used to make something look more attractive. Favor causes people to be attracted to you.

Isaiah 28:5 says, "In that day shall the Lord of hosts be for a crown of glory, and for a diadem of beauty, unto the residue of his people" (KJV). Favor releases a diadem of beauty. Beauty is connected to favor. We can have more favor as we walk in the beauty of holiness. Beauty is glory and majesty. Our God is a god of glory, beauty, and majesty.

A crown is like a hat or turban, whereas the diadem is the most beautiful, glorious part of the crown. It is the headband. Generally speaking, a crown signifies glory, but its beauty is in the band, which may be full of jewels and precious stones. The diadem, or headband, is the beauty of the glorious crown. (See also Psalm 90:17; 96:9.)

To be crowned with favor means to be under God's favor. The crown sits on the head. What is on the head flows down to the rest of the body. The crown also represents power and authority. Favor will promote you and bring you to a place of power, authority, glory, and honor.

The foolish can't expect to receive from the Lord. But if you make wisdom a priority, favor will follow.

Prayers for the Wisdom of God

Lord, teach me wisdom's ways and lead me in straight paths (Prov. 4:11).

The Lord's wisdom will save my life (Eccles. 7:12).

I pray for an understanding heart that is enshrined in wisdom (Prov. 14:33).

I tune my ears to Your wisdom, Lord, and concentrate on understanding (Prov. 2:2, NLT).

I do not put my trust in human wisdom "but in the power of God" (1 Cor. 2:5).

In You, O Lord, lie the hidden treasures of wisdom and knowledge (Col. 2:3).

I listen when those who are older speak, for wisdom comes with age (Job 32:7).

Lord, Your wisdom is more profitable than silver, and its wages are better than gold (Prov. 3:14).

Let wisdom multiply my days and add years to my life (Prov. 9:11).

Let my house be built by wisdom and become strong through good sense (Prov. 24:3).

I will not be foolish and trust my own insight, but I will walk in wisdom and be safe (Prov. 28:26).

Let the fruit of my life prove Your wisdom is right (Luke 7:35).

Let the fear of the Lord teach me wisdom (Prov. 15:33).

I will obey Your commands, so that I will grow in wisdom (Ps. 111:10).

Fill me with Your Spirit, O God, and give me great wisdom, ability, and expertise in all kinds of crafts (Exod. 31:3).

Lord, give me wisdom and knowledge to lead effectively (2 Chron. 1:10).

Let those who have gone before me teach me wisdom of old (Job 8:8–10).

True wisdom and power are found in You, God (Job 12:13).

The price of Your wisdom, O Lord, cannot be purchased with jewels mounted in fine gold; its price is far above rubies (Job 28:17–18).

I will keep silent, O God. Teach me wisdom (Job 33:33).

Your wisdom will save me from evil people and from the immoral woman (Prov. 2:12, 16).

I will embrace Your wisdom, for it is happiness and a tree of life to me (Prov. 3:18).

I will pay attention to Your wisdom, O Lord. I will listen carefully to Your wise counsel (Prov. 5:1).

Give me understanding so that Your knowledge and wisdom will come easily to me (Prov. 14:6).

Grant me wisdom so that I may also have good judgment, knowledge, and discernment (Prov. 8:12).

Thank You, Lord, that You will certainly give me the wisdom and knowledge I requested (2 Chron. 1:12).

I will not be impressed with my own wisdom, but I will instead fear the Lord and turn away from evil (Prov. 3:7).

I will not turn my back on Your wisdom, O God, for it will protect and guard me (Prov. 4:6).

Your "wisdom is better than strength" (Eccles. 9:16).

I thank and praise You, God of my ancestors, for You have given me wisdom and strength (Dan. 2:23, NLT).

For You will give me the right words and such wisdom that none of my opponents will be able to reply or refute me (Luke 21:15).

I need wisdom; therefore, I will ask my generous God, and He will give it to me. He will not rebuke me for asking (Jas. 1:5).

I pray that my life pleases You, O God, that You might grant me "wisdom, knowledge, and joy" (Eccles. 2:26).

WISDOM CONFESSIONS

I receive the wisdom of God and the fear of the Lord. Let them be a part of my life.

I want to make wise decisions.

I want to know the Word of God.

Wisdom is my companion. She will bless me, promote me, protect me, and exalt me.

I receive wisdom, the wisdom of the Word, the Spirit of wisdom.

I receive the wisdom of heaven to walk on the earth.

I will not make foolish decisions.

I will not make foolish choices.

I will not have foolish relationships.

Lord, teach me wisdom's ways and lead me in a straight path (Prov. 4:11).

I want to walk in wisdom all the days of my life, and I am blessed in Jesus' name.

I pray for an understanding heart that is enshrined in wisdom (Prov. 14:33, NLT).

I tune my ears to Your wisdom, Lord, and concentrate on understanding (Prov. 2:2, NLT).

I do not put my trust in human wisdom but in the power of God (1 Cor. 2:5).

In You, O Lord, lie the hidden treasures of wisdom and knowledge (Col. 2:3).

I listen when those who are older speak, for wisdom comes with age (Job 32:7).

Lord, Your wisdom is more profitable than silver, and its wages are better than gold (Prov. 3:14).

Let wisdom multiply my days and add years to my life (Prov. 9:11).

Let my house be built by wisdom and become strong through good sense (Prov. 24:3).

I will not be foolish and trust my own insight, but I will walk in wisdom and be safe (Prov. 28:26).

Let the fruit of my life prove Your wisdom is right (Luke 7:35).

I will obey Your commands, so I will grow in wisdom (Ps. 111:10).

Fill me with Your Spirit, O God, and give me great wisdom, ability, and expertise in all kinds of crafts (Exod. 31:3).

Lord, give me wisdom and knowledge to lead effectively (2 Chron. 1:10).

Let those who have gone before me teach me wisdom of old (Job 8:8–10).

The price of Your wisdom, O Lord, cannot be purchased with jewels mounted in fine gold; its price is far above rubies (Job 28:17–18).

Your wisdom will save me from evil people and from the immoral woman (Prov. 2:12, 16).

I will embrace Your wisdom, for it is happiness and a tree of life (Prov. 3:18).

I pay attention to Your wisdom, O Lord. I listen carefully to Your wise counsel (Prov. 5:1, NLT).

Give me understanding so that Your knowledge and wisdom will come easily to me (Prov. 14:6).

Grant me wisdom so I may have good judgment, knowledge, and discernment (Prov. 8:12, NLT).

Thank You, Lord, for certainly giving me the wisdom and knowledge I have requested (2 Chron. 1:12, NLT).

I will not be impressed with their own wisdom, but they will fear the Lord and turn away from evil (Prov. 3:7, NLT).

I will not turn my back on Your wisdom, O God, for it will protect and guard me (Prov. 4:6, NLT).

I thank and praise You, God of my ancestors, for You have given me wisdom and strength (Dan. 2:23, NLT).

You will give me "the right words and such wisdom that none of my opponents will be able to reply or refute it" (Luke 21:15, NLT).

I need wisdom; therefore, I will ask my generous God, and He will give it to me. He will not rebuke me for asking (Jas. 1:5, NLT).

I pray that my life pleases You, O God, that You might grant me wisdom, knowledge, and joy (Eccles. 2:26, NLT).

Chapter 3

HUMILITY—THE FAVOR MAGNET

But he giveth more grace [favor]. Wherefore he saith,
God resisteth the proud, but giveth grace [favor] to
the humble.

—James 4:6, kjv

I F YOU WANT to enjoy God's favor, it is absolutely necessary that you walk in humility. God resists the proud,
but shows grace, mercy, and favor to the humble. Those
who are humble depend on the grace and favor of God.
The humble know they cannot succeed without God's
favor. The humble recognize their need for God's favor.
While we all say we want the favor of God, we need to
examine ourselves to make sure we are not repelling the
favor of God.

Pride is one of the most difficult demons to defeat. In Job
41, pride is manifested as the spirit of Leviathan, a ruling
spirit that causes people to be stubborn and stiff-necked (v.
22). Job 41 says Leviathan's scales are his pride. No air can
come between them. Air represents spirit, and one of the
manifestations of pride is the inability to flow in the Spirit.
When we are proud, rebellious, and unwilling to submit to

the authority of God, we limit the flow of the Spirit and cut ourselves off from receiving God's favor.

The Bible says the Israelites could not go into the Promised Land because they were stiff-necked, stubborn, and disobedient. That whole generation died in the wilderness. When forty years had passed, Joshua and Caleb and the new generation of God's people went in. God does not give His promises to stiff-necked, stubborn, rebellious, hard-hearted, proud, disobedient people. It does not work. It will never work.

The Scriptures tell us again and again that humility attracts the favor of God.

> I show special favor to the humble and contrite, who respect what I have to say.
>
> —ISAIAH 66:2, NET

> I will look favorably on this kind of person: one who is humble, submissive in spirit, and trembles at my word.
>
> —ISAIAH 66:2, CSB

> For God sets Himself against the proud (the insolent, the overbearing, the disdainful, the presumptuous, the boastful)—[and He opposes, frustrates, and defeats them], but gives grace (favor, blessing) to the humble.
>
> —1 PETER 5:5, AMPC

God opposes the arrogant but favors the humble.

—1 PETER 5:5, GW

Humble yourselves in the sight of the Lord, and he will lift you up.

—JAMES 4:10

Pride will cause you to lose the favor of God. Saul rebelled and lost favor. Israel rebelled and lost favor. Pride and rebellion will repel the favor of God from your life. Again, God resists the proud but gives grace (favor) to the humble.

FASTING LEADS TO HUMILITY

Fasting has always been a way to seek the help of God during times of crisis, but it is also a way to attract the favor of God. Psalm 35:13 connects fasting with humility: "But as for me, when they were sick, my clothing was sack cloth: I humbled my soul with fasting; and my prayer returned into mine own bosom" (KJV). You can humble your soul through fasting, and as your soul is humbled, you attract the favor of God.

We also see humility attached to favor in Isaiah 58, where the Lord promises that great favor is released through fasting.

Then shall thy light break forth as the morning, and thine health shall spring forth speedily: and thy righteousness shall go before thee; the glory of the LORD shall be thy reward. Then shalt thou call, and the LORD shall answer; thou shalt cry, and he shall say, Here I am. If thou take away from the midst of thee the yoke, the putting forth of the finger, and speaking vanity.

—Isaiah 58:8–9, KJV

That thou appear not unto men to fast, but unto thy Father which is in secret: and thy Father, which seeth in secret, shall reward thee openly.

—Matthew 6:18, KJV

HUMILITY, SUBMISSION, AND FAVOR

Many would not connect favor to submission, but they are related. Submission is a sign of humility. This also means that submission as a manifestation of humility is a key to favor. Let's look at three levels of submission that God requires.

Submit to God.

James 4:7 tells us that our first submission is to God: "Submit yourselves therefore to God. Resist the devil, and he will flee from you" (KJV).

Submit to others.

In 1 Peter 5:5 we are also told to submit to one another: "Likewise, ye younger, submit yourselves unto the elder. Yea, all of you be subject one to another, and be clothed with humility: for God resisteth the proud, and giveth grace to the humble" (KJV). This principle is a problem for many who claim submission to God only and are unable to submit appropriately to those around them.

This verse also shows that we are to be clothed (or covered) with humility. We should wear humility like a garment. As we humbly submit to one another, we attract the favor of God. (See Ephesians 5:21.)

Submit to leaders.

> Obey them that have the rule over you, and submit yourselves: for they watch for your souls, as they that must give account, that they may do it with joy, and not with grief: for that is unprofitable for you.
>
> —HEBREWS 13:17, KJV

We see this principle throughout the Scriptures: David was submitted to Saul. Joseph was submitted to Potiphar. Ruth submitted herself to Naomi. Daniel was submitted to the king. Esther submitted herself to Mordecai. Samuel was submitted to Eli. All these men and women of God received great favor, proving how important it is to honor the leadership God has placed within His body. God favors those who respect His servants and sent ones.

> He that receiveth a prophet in the name of a prophet shall receive a prophet's reward; and he that

receiveth a righteous man in the name of a righteous man shall receive a righteous man's reward.

—MATTHEW 10:41, KJV

God rewards and favors those who bless and favor His sent ones. Don't dishonor His servants if you want God's favor. I am not referring to controlling leaders, but leaders who walk in love and serve God's people.

In Philippians 4:19 Paul gave a promise to the Philippians after they supported and blessed his ministry. He told them, "My God shall supply all your need according to his riches in glory by Christ Jesus" (KJV). You get favor when you bless men and women of God.

Luke tells about the women who followed Jesus and ministered to Him from their substance:

> And it came to pass afterward, that he went throughout every city and village, preaching and shewing the glad tidings of the kingdom of God: and the twelve were with him, and certain women, which had been healed of evil spirits and infirmities, Mary called Magdalene, out of whom went seven devils, and Joanna the wife of Chuza Herod's steward, and Susanna, and many others, which ministered unto him of their substance.
>
> —LUKE 8:1–3, KJV

There is great favor when you bless those who have ministered to you and blessed you.

Pride will cut the flow of favor from your life. As we resist pride and walk in humility, we will see the favor of God poured out on our lives.

PRAYERS THAT BREAK THE SPIRIT OF PRIDE

The Lord is above the spirit of the proud (Exod. 18:11).

The Lord will break the power of pride; He will make my heavens like iron and my earth like bronze (Lev. 26:19).

I will not talk proudly and will let no arrogance come from my mouth (1 Sam. 2:3).

Like King Hezekiah, let prideful leaders humble themselves so that the wrath of the Lord does not come upon the people (2 Chron. 32:26).

Thank You, Lord, that You turn me from my deeds and conceal my pride from me so that my soul may be kept back from the pit and my life from perishing by the sword (Job 33:17–18).

Lord, I break the spirit of pride. Please answer when I cry out (Job 35:12).

Let that spirit be caught in the plots it has devised (Ps. 10:2).

The Lord will bring down haughty looks (Ps. 18:27).

"Let not the foot of pride come against me, and let not the hand of the wicked drive me away" (Ps. 36:11, NKJV).

I do not respect the proud or those who turn aside to lies. I make the Lord my trust (Ps. 40:4).

Pride will not serve as my necklace, nor will violence cover me like a garment (Ps. 73:6).

The Lord will not endure "a haughty look and a proud heart" (Ps. 101:5). "Lord, my heart is not haughty" (Ps. 131:1).

I fear the Lord; therefore I hate evil, pride, arrogance, and the evil way. I hate the perverse mouth (Prov. 8:13).

I rebuke the shame that comes from a spirit of pride (Prov. 11:2).

The proud in heart are an abomination to the Lord. Let them not go unpunished (Prov. 16:5).

I break the spirit of pride, so that I will not fall and be destroyed (Prov. 16:18).

I come against the spirit of the proud and haughty man who acts with arrogant pride (Prov. 21:24).

I will not be wise in my own eyes (Prov. 26:12).

I will let another man praise me, and not my own mouth; a stranger, and not my own lips (Prov. 27:2).

I break the spirit of pride. It will not bring me low. I will have a humble spirit (Prov. 29:23).

Let the Lord halt the arrogance of the proud and lay low the haughtiness of the terrible (Isa. 13:11).

I break the pride of Moab. It shall no longer be proud of its haughtiness, pride, and wrath. The lies it speaks will not be so (Isa. 16:6).

Lord, bring dishonor to the spirit of pride (Isa. 23:9).

As a swimmer reaches out to swim, Lord, spread out Your hands in their midst and bring down the prideful and their trickery (Isa. 25:11).

Let the crown of pride, the drunkards of Ephraim, be trampled underfoot (Isa. 28:3).

May the Lord ruin "the pride of Judah and the great pride of Jerusalem" (Jer. 13:9).

Hear and give ear, spirit of pride. The Lord has spoken (Jer. 13:15).

Let the proud stumble and fall, and no one raise him up. Let the Lord kindle a fire in his cities, and it will devour all around him (Jer. 50:32).

Those who uphold Egypt will fall; the pride of her power will come down, and those within her shall fall by the sword (Ezek. 30:6).

Those who walk in pride will be put down by the King of heaven (Dan. 4:37).

I break pride off of my life in the name of Jesus. I will not stumble in my iniquity as Israel, Ephraim, and Judah did (Hos. 5:5).

The spirit of pride will not rule me. I shall not be desolate in the day of rebuke (Hos. 5:9).

Let them not testify to His face then go on not returning to the Lord their God (Hos. 7:10).

Let all their cities and everything in them be given to their enemies (Amos 6:8).

Let not the pride of my heart deceive me. I have been brought low to the ground (Obad. 3).

The spirit of pride will not cause me to be scattered (Luke 1:51).

I dare not class myself or compare myself with those who commend themselves. They are not wise (2 Cor. 10:12).

I will not be puffed up with pride and fall into the same condemnation as the devil (1 Tim. 3:6).

The Lord resists the proud. Let me be like the humble one who receives grace from God (Jas. 4:6).

I break the spirit of the pride of life, for it is not of the Father but is of the world (1 John 2:16).

PRAYERS AGAINST LEVIATHAN

In the name of Jesus, I break all curses of pride and Leviathan from my life.

Bring down the proud demons that have exalted themselves against Your people.

God, You resist the proud (Jas. 4:6). Your power is against the high ones who have rebelled against You.

Break the pride of Leviathan's power (Lev. 26:19).

Raise up a watch over Leviathan (Job 7:12).

Smite through Leviathan with Your understanding (Job 26:12, KJV).

Cast abroad the rage of Your wrath and abase Leviathan (Job 40:11, KJV).

Look on Leviathan and bring him low. Tread him down in his place (Job 40:12).

Break the teeth of Leviathan and pluck the spoil out of his mouth (Job 29:17; 41:14, KJV).

I strip the scales of Leviathan and take away his armor (Job 41:15; Luke 11:22).

"Let not the foot of pride come against me" (Ps. 36:11, KJV).

O Lord, break "the heads of the dragons in the waters" (Ps. 74:13, KJV).

Crush the heads of Leviathan in pieces (Ps. 74:14).

O Lord, render to Leviathan what he deserves (Ps. 94:2).

Let not Leviathan oppress me (Ps. 119:122).

Let not the proud waters go over my soul (Ps. 124:5, KJV).

I rebuke and destroy every trap the devil has set for me (Ps. 140:5, NLT).

"Punish Leviathan the piercing serpent, even Leviathan that crooked serpent," with Your fierce, great, and strong sword (Isa. 27:1, KJV).

Break "the crown of pride" (Isa. 28:1, KJV).

Let the waters of the deep be dried up, and destroy every spirit of Leviathan (Isa. 44:27).

Let the proud spirits stumble and fall (Jer. 50:32).

I call for a drought upon Leviathan's waters (Jer. 50:38; 51:36).

PRAYERS AND DECLARATIONS OF THE HUMBLE

I will humble myself in the sight of the Lord, and He will lift me up (Jas. 4:10).

I will not allow pride to enter my heart and cause me shame. I will be humble and clothed in wisdom (Prov. 11:2).

I am better off being of a humble spirit with the lowly than dividing the spoil with the proud (Prov. 16:19).

I will humble myself under the mighty hand of God that He may exalt me in due time (1 Pet. 5:6).

"My soul will make its boast in the LORD; the humble will hear of it and be glad" (Ps. 34:2).

I will not be like Amon, but I will humble myself before the Lord and will not trespass more and more (2 Chron. 33:23, KJV).

Lord, humble me and test me that I might do good in the end (Deut. 8:16, NLT).

Let me be like Moses, who was very humble, more than all the men who were on the face of the earth (Num. 12:3).

I will submit myself to my elders. I will be clothed in humility, and God will give me grace (1 Pet. 5:5).

I will speak evil of no one. I will be peaceable and gentle, showing all humility to all men (Titus 3:2).

"As the elect of God, holy and beloved," I will "put on tender mercies, kindness, humility, meekness, and longsuffering" (Col. 3:12, NKJV).

I will seek the Lord. I will seek righteousness and humility so that I may be hidden on the day of the Lord's anger (Zeph. 2:3).

I will do what the Lord requires of me: I will do justly, love mercy, and walk humbly with my God (Mic. 6:8).

I desire to be like Christ, who "humbled Himself and became obedient to the point of death, even the death of the cross" (Phil. 2:8, NKJV).

Through humility and the fear of the Lord I am given riches and honor and life (Prov. 22:4).

I will humble myself as a little child (Matt. 18:4).

CHAPTER 4

GENEROSITY—THE KEY TO ABUNDANT FAVOR

A good man sheweth favour, and lendeth.

—PSALM 112:5, KJV

GIVING IS ONE of the ways you show favor to others and tap into the favor of God.

The Bible teaches a very simple message about being blessed to be a blessing. It is a cyclical law much like sowing and reaping. In Christian circles it has been called the law of the harvest; in the world, karma; and in science, cause and effect: "What goes around comes around." "You get what you pay for." "You get out what you put in." "Whatever you sow, you will reap."

Regardless of what man has tried to label it, this law of giving and receiving originated with God at the foundation of the world. It is not a hypothesis or theory. It is an ingrained law that applies to life on this earth and in heaven whether we are aware of it or not.

What you release will be given back to you; and even more, you will receive in proportion to how you give. If you give (or sow) sparingly, you will receive (or reap) sparingly (2 Cor. 9:6).

A blessed and favored Christian is vibrant, fruitful, and able to give and sustain life. But if all you do is receive, receive, receive, you will end up like the Dead Sea—becoming too salty and too toxic to support any kind of life. So if you want to receive the blessing and favor of God, you have to be ready to give.

There is one type of giving I want to emphasize that will cause favor to be multiplied to you in ways you may have never experienced. This type of giving will bring you into a realm of favor that no other type of giving will.

> And God is able to make all grace [favor] abound toward you [superabound]; that ye, always having all sufficiency in all things, may abound to every good work: (As it is written, He hath *dispersed abroad*; he hath given to the poor: his righteousness remaineth for ever.)
> —2 CORINTHIANS 9:8–9, KJV, EMPHASIS ADDED

I have emphasized "dispersed abroad." Years ago the Lord challenged our ministry to sow into other nations. He wanted us to disperse abroad. An abundance of favor is released to a ministry that disperses abroad. God will make favor "superabound" toward you. This is the literal meaning of the word *abound* in the Greek language. There will come a superabundance of favor.

Most believers have never walked in this level of favor, but it is available to those who will disperse abroad. Showing mercy and giving to poor nations is the way to tap into this realm of favor.

An abundance of financial favor will be released to them who disperse abroad. God will multiply your sown seed. This is how you can enter into the realm of multiplication. Multiplication always brings abundance.

Stinginess will choke the flow of favor out of your life. You cannot be stingy and have an abundance of favor. Givers receive favor. "Give and it shall be given unto you, good measure, pressed down, and shaken together, and running over [overflowing], shall men give into your bosom" (Luke 6:38, KJV). People will favor you by giving into your bosom. There will be so much favor that your finances will overflow. This is an abundance of favor, and it is the level we want to walk and live in.

THE REALM OF MEGA-FAVOR

The Greek word *megas* means "great,"[1] and from it we get the English word *mega*. In other words, the apostles had mega-grace. Mega means great or large; it also means "million."[2] There are megabucks, megabytes, mega doses, and megahertz. The implication is always something huge. We want to enter the realm of mega-favor.

The apostles' anointing releases great favor. This is a part of the apostolic church. There is no lack when this level of favor is present.

> I thank my God always on your behalf, for the grace [favor] of God which is given you by Jesus Christ; that in everything ye are enriched by him, in all utterance, and in all knowledge; even as the testimony of Christ was confirmed in you: So that ye come behind in no gift; waiting for the coming of our Lord Jesus Christ.
>
> —1 CORINTHIANS 1:4–7, KJV

This is great favor. When you walk in this realm of favor, you will "come behind in no gift" (1 Cor. 1:7, KJV), meaning you will lack no spiritual gift. You will be enriched in everything. To *enrich* means "to make rich."[3] To *be* rich means to have an abundant supply.[4] This is a level of favor that releases abundance.

Notice that the apostles would release grace when writing to the churches. There is an anointing upon apostles and other ministry gifts to release favor to the body of Christ. Favor (grace) and apostleship are linked together (Rom. 1:5).

This is the hour in which God is restoring apostolic ministry to the church. The church is again receiving the ministry of the apostles. Apostles are once again being recognized. As we embrace true apostolic ministers, we will see a great release of God's favor to the church. This is already happening. It is the time of God's favor. This is the year of the Lord's favor.

> Thou shalt arise, and have mercy upon Zion: for the time to favour her, yea, the set time, is come.
>
> —PSALM 102:13, KJV

We are living in an apostolic time. This is a season of favor. God is doing some awesome things in this season. He is doing a work so great that it will not be believed (Hab. 1:5). It is a set time. This means that it has been ordained by the Father. No devil can stop it. You must believe it and receive God's favor.

PRAYERS FOR THE BLESSING OF GIVING

"It is more blessed to give than to receive" (Acts 20:35).

I give, and it is given to me; "pressed down, shaken together, and running over, will men give unto" me (Luke 6:38).

I sow bountifully, and I reap bountifully (2 Cor. 9:6).

Lord, remember all my offerings (Ps. 20:3).

I honor You with the first fruits of my increase; therefore, let my barns be filled with plenty (Prov. 3:9–10).

I will not lack; I am a giver (Ps. 34:10).

Let wealth and riches be in my house, for I am a giver (Ps. 112:3).

I bring the tithe and offerings to the storehouse. Let the windows of heaven be opened over my life (Mal. 3:10).

I bring the tithe and offerings to the storehouse. Rebuke the devourer for my sake (Mal. 3:10–11).

I sow into good ground, and I reap an abundant harvest (Gal. 6:7).

I believe in seedtime and harvest as long as the earth remains (Gen. 8:22).

I give, so release Your heaps into my life (2 Chron. 31:8, KJV).

I have a bountiful eye, and I give; therefore, I receive Your blessing (Prov. 22:9).

I give; therefore, give me richly all things to enjoy (1 Tim. 6:17).

I will bring an offering and come into Your courts (Ps. 96:8).

Never again will I hold back from giving, for I give, and it is given to me, "good measure, pressed down, shaken together, and running over" do men give to me (Luke 6:38).

Never again will I allow fear to stop me from giving.

Never again will I allow doubt and unbelief to stop me from believing in the promises of God (Heb. 3:19).

Let my prayers and giving come up as a memorial before You (Acts 10:4).

I will support anointed ministers, and my needs are met according to Your riches in glory (Phil. 4:18–19).

I will minister to You, Lord, with my substance (Luke 8:2–3, KJV).

I am a doer of the Word, and I obey Your Word by giving (Jas. 1:22; Luke 6:38).

Let my giving and tithes increase (Deut. 14:22, KJV).

Let my latter end greatly increase (Job 8:7).

I will flourish like a palm tree and grow like a cedar in Lebanon (Ps. 92:12).

NEVER AGAIN CONFESSIONS THAT BLOCK THIEVES OF SUCCESS AND PROSPERITY

Never again will I allow poverty and lack to control my life, for my God supplies all my "need according to His riches in glory by Christ Jesus" (Phil. 4:19).

Never again will I lack, for I have plenty (Gen. 27:28).

Never again will I lack, for I will have plenty of silver (Job 22:25, KJV).

Never again will I lack; I will be plenteous in goods (Deut. 28:11, KJV).

Never again will I lack, but I will prosper through prophetic ministry (Ezra 6:14).

Never again will I sow and not reap, but I will reap where others have sown (John 4:38).

Never again will I carry a bag full of holes (Hag. 1:6).

Never again will I be poor, for the Lord became poor that I through His poverty might be rich (2 Cor. 8:9).

Never again will I live without the desires of my heart because I will delight myself in the Lord (Ps. 37:4).

Never again will I allow covetousness to control my life, but I am a liberal giver (Prov. 11:25, KJV).

Never again will the enemy devour my finances, for the Lord has rebuked the devourer for my sake (Mal. 3:11).

Never again will I hold back from giving, for I give, and it is given to me; "good measure, pressed down, shaken together, and running over" do men give to me (Luke 6:38).

Never again will I allow fear to stop me from giving.

Never again will I allow debt to control my life, for I will "lend unto many nations" and not borrow (Deut. 28:12, KJV), for "the borrower is servant to the lender" (Prov. 22:7).

Never again will I allow doubt and unbelief to stop me from believing in the promises of God (Heb. 3:19).

Never again will I think poverty and lack, for as a man thinks in his heart, so is he (Prov. 23:7).

Never again will my basket and store be empty, for my basket and store are blessed (Deut. 28:5, KJV).

Never again will I allow slothfulness and laziness to dominate my life, for slothfulness casts into a deep sleep (Prov. 19:15, KJV).

Never again will I allow Satan to steal my finances, but I have abundant life (John 10:10).

Never again will I limit what God can do in my finances and in my life (Ps. 78:41, KJV).

Never again will I tolerate lack, for my God gives me "abundance of all things" (Deut. 28:47).

Never again will I have just enough, for El Shaddai gives me more than enough (Gen. 17:1–2, NLT).

Never again will I use my money for sinful things (Ezek. 16:17).

Never again will the enemy hold back my blessings.

Never again will I doubt God's desire to prosper me, for the Lord takes pleasure in the prosperity of His servant (Ps. 35:27, KJV).

Never again will I be the tail and not the head (Deut. 28:13).

Never again will I be a borrower and not a lender (Deut. 28:12).

Never again will I be behind and not in front (Deut. 25:18).

Never again will I believe I don't have power to get wealth, for God gives me power to get wealth to establish His covenant (Deut. 8:18).

Never again will I lack any good thing, because I will seek the Lord (Ps. 34:10).

Never again will I lack prosperity, but whatever I do will prosper, because I delight in the law of the Lord (Ps. 1:2–3).

Never again will I lack anointing for my head (Eccles. 9:8, NIV).

Never again will I allow the circumstances to steal my joy, for the joy of the Lord is my strength (Neh. 8:10).

Never again will I lack favor for my life, for with favor the Lord will surround me as a shield (Ps. 5:12).

Never again will I walk in the flesh instead of walking in the Spirit (Gal. 5:16).

Never again will I allow my flesh to do what it wants. I am crucified with Christ (Gal. 2:20).

Never again will I walk in the works of the flesh, but I will manifest the fruit of the Spirit (Gal. 5:22–23).

Never again will I be weak, for I am strong (Joel 3:10, KJV).

Never again will I be oppressed, for I am "far from oppression" (Isa. 54:14, KJV).

Never again will I be vexed and tormented by demons, for I

have been delivered from the power of darkness and translated into the kingdom of God's dear Son (Col. 1:13, KJV).

Never again will I allow perversion and sexual immorality to control my life; I flee fornication (1 Cor. 6:18, KJV).

Never again will I enjoy that which is unclean and forbidden by the Lord (2 Cor. 6:17).

Never again will I allow worldliness and carnality to control my life (1 John 2:15).

Never again will I conform to the world (Rom. 12:2).

Never again will I allow anger to control my life, but I am slow to anger and sin not (Prov. 16:32; Jas. 1:19).

Never again will I get angry at another person's success, but I rejoice in the success of others (Rom. 12:10, 15).

Never again will I allow unforgiveness and bitterness to control my life (Eph. 4:31).

Never again will I allow discouragement and depression to dominate my life, but I will praise Him who is the help of my countenance (Ps. 42:5, KJV).

Never again will I allow jealousy and envy to enter my heart, for envy is the rottenness of the bones (Prov. 14:30).

ABUNDANCE AND PROSPERITY CONFESSIONS

I will prosper and be in health as my soul prospers (3 John 2, NKJV).

I will not lack, for You are my shepherd, and I will not want (Ps. 23:1).

Lord, prosper me and let me have abundance.

Lord, You are El Shaddai, the God of more than enough; give me everything I need to fulfill my destiny, and let me have more than I need (Gen. 17, NLT).

Lord, You became poor that through Your poverty I might be rich (2 Cor. 8:9).

Lord, let me not lack any good thing, for I delight myself in You (Ps. 119:16, 47, NKJV).

Lord, give me the desires of my heart, for I seek You (Ps. 37:4).

Lord, I put first Your kingdom and Your righteousness, and all things are added to me (Matt. 6:33).

Lord, bless my coming in and my going out (Ps. 121:8).

Lord, let me be blessed in the city and blessed in the field (Deut. 28:3).

Lord, let me be blessed to be above and not beneath (Deut. 28:13).

Lord, let me be blessed to be the head and not the tail (Deut. 28:13).

Lord, let me be blessed with dominion and victory over the enemy (Ps. 119:133).

Lord, let everything my hand touches be blessed.

Lord, let Your blessing overtake my life.

Lord, let Your favor bless my life.

Lord, command Your blessing on my storehouse.

Lord, command Your blessing, even life evermore, on my life.

Lord, let me have plenty of silver.

Lord, multiply Your grace in my life, and let me abound to every good work (2 Cor. 9:8).

Lord, let me have abundance and not scarceness.

Lord, let there be no holes in my bag (Hag. 1:6).

Let the windows of heaven be opened over my life and pour me out a blessing I don't have room enough to receive. Lord, rebuke the devourer for my sake (Mal. 3:10–11).

Lord, I seek You; cause me to prosper (2 Chron. 26:5, kjv).

Lord, speak over my life and let me prosper.

Lord, send Your angel and prosper my way (Gen. 24:40).

Lord, be with me and let me be a prosperous person (Gen. 39:2).

Let me have wisdom and prosperity (1 Kings 10:7).

Lord God of heaven, prosper me (Neh. 2:20).

Lord, take pleasure in my prosperity (Ps. 35:27, KJV).

Lord, send prosperity to my life (Ps. 118:25, KJV).

Let peace and prosperity be within my house (Ps. 122:7).

Let the gifts You have given me bring prosperity (Prov. 17:8).

Lord, You have called me; make my way prosperous (Isa. 48:15).

Lord, rule and reign over my life with prosperity (Jer. 23:5).

Lord, procure Your goodness and prosperity in my life (Jer. 33:9).

Lord, bless me, and let me not forget prosperity (Lam. 3:17).

Lord, let me prosper like Abraham (Gen. 24:35).

Lord, bless me and increase me like Abraham my father (Isa. 51:2).

Lord, let me prosper like Joseph (Gen. 39:2).

Lord, bless me like Asher, and let me dip my feet in oil (Deut. 33:24).

Lord, bless my house like the house of Obed-Edom (2 Sam. 6:12).

Lord, bless me and bring me into a wealthy place (Ps. 66:12, KJV).

Lord, give me power to get wealth (Deut. 8:18, KJV).

Lord, I am a giver; let wealth and riches be in my house (Ps. 112:3).

Lord, Your blessing makes rich, and You add no sorrow (Prov. 10:22).

Lord, bless me with enough to eat, with plenty left (2 Chron. 31:10).

Lord, let me prosper like Daniel (Dan. 6:28).

Let every journey I take be prosperous (Rom. 1:10, KJV).

Let every good seed I plant prosper (Zech. 8:12).

CHAPTER 5

KNOWLEDGE—THE FAVOR MULTIPLIER

Grace [favor] and peace be multiplied unto you through the knowledge of God, and of Jesus our Lord.
—2 PETER 1:2, KJV

FAVOR IS NOT only unlocked but also multiplied through the knowledge of God and of Jesus our Lord. This means that as we increase in the knowledge of God and the Lord Jesus, we increase in favor. Because favor is multiplied through knowledge, I always encourage the saints to read good books and study the Word of God. Learn more about the things of God. Associate with wise people. When you increase in knowledge, you will also increase in favor.

Ignorance will stop the flow of favor, so don't remain in ignorance. Second Peter 3:18 tells us to "grow in the grace and knowledge of our Lord and Savior Jesus Christ." Study, read, and learn. Listen to good messages. Attend a church where the Word of God is being taught. Associate with people who know God. Knowledge is a spirit (Isa.

11:2). The spirit of knowledge will be imparted unto you as you associate with people who really know God.

We want to get into the realm of favor where it is multiplied. Multiplication brings tremendous increase. This is God's desire for you. He wants to multiply His favor in your life. When you increase in knowledge, He will multiply His favor unto you.

When favor is multiplied, you will begin to have an abundance of favor, and the work of your hands will be fruitful. You will then be able to reign in life.

PRAYERS FOR REVELATION

You are a God that reveals secrets. Lord, reveal Your secrets unto me (Dan. 2:28).

Reveal to me "the deep and secret things" (Dan. 2:22).

Let me understand things kept secret from the foundation of the world (Matt. 13:35).

Let the seals be broken from Your Word (Dan. 12:9).

Let me understand and have revelation of Your will and purpose for my life.

Give me the spirit of wisdom and revelation, and let the eyes of my understanding be enlightened (Eph. 1:17–18).

Let me understand heavenly things (John 3:12).

Open my eyes to behold wondrous things out of Your Word (Ps. 119:18).

Let me know and understand the mysteries of the kingdom (Mark 4:11, KJV).

Let me speak to others by revelation (1 Cor. 14:6).

Reveal Your secrets to Your servants the prophets (Amos 3:7).

Let the hidden things be made manifest (Mark 4:22).

Hide Your truths from the wise and prudent, and reveal them to babes (Matt. 11:25, KJV).

Let Your arm be revealed in my life (John 12:38).

Reveal the things that belong to me (Deut. 29:29).

Let Your Word be revealed unto me (1 Sam. 3:7).

Let Your glory be revealed in my life (Isa. 40:5).

Let Your righteousness be revealed in my life (Isa. 56:1).

Let me receive visions and revelations of the Lord (2 Cor. 12:1).

Let me receive an abundance of revelations (2 Cor. 12:7).

Let me be a good steward of Your mysteries (1 Cor. 4:1).

Let me "speak the mystery of Christ" (Col. 4:3).

Let me receive and understand Your hidden wisdom (1 Cor. 2:7).

Hide not Your commandments from me (Ps. 119:19).

Let me "speak the wisdom of God in a mystery" (1 Cor. 2:7).

Let me "make known the mystery of the gospel" (Eph. 6:19).

Make known unto me the mystery of Your will (Eph. 1:9).

Open Your "dark sayings upon the harp" (Ps. 49:4, KJV).

Let me understand Your parables; "the words of the wise and their dark sayings" (Prov. 1:6, KJV).

Lord, light my candle and enlighten my darkness (Ps. 18:28, KJV).

Make darkness light before me (Isa. 42:16).

Give me "the treasures of darkness and hidden riches of secret places" (Isa. 45:3).

Let Your candle shine upon my head (Job 29:3, KJV).

My spirit is "the candle of the LORD, searching all the inward parts of the belly" (Prov. 20:27, KJV).

Let me understand "the deep things of God" (1 Cor. 2:10).

Let me understand Your deep thoughts (Ps. 92:5).

Let my eyes be enlightened with Your Word (Ps. 19:8).

My eyes are blessed to see (Luke 10:23).

Let all spiritual cataracts and scales be removed from my eyes (Acts 9:18).

Let me "comprehend with all saints what is the breadth and length and depth and height" of Your love (Eph. 3:18).

Let my reins instruct me in the night season, and let me awaken with revelation (Ps. 16:7, KJV).

CONFESSIONS FOR MEDITATING ON THE WORD

I will meditate also of all the Lord's work and talk of His doings (Ps. 77:12, KJV).

I will meditate on the Lord's precepts and contemplate His ways (Ps. 119:15, NKJV).

Princes also sit and speak against me, but I meditate on the Lord's statutes (Ps. 119:23, NKJV).

"Let the proud be ashamed; for they dealt perversely with me without a cause, but I will meditate on thy precepts" (Ps. 119:78, KJV).

My eyes are awake during the night watches that I may meditate on the Lord's Word (Ps. 119:148).

"I remember the days of old; I meditate on all thy works; I muse on the work of thy hands" (Ps. 143:5, KJV).

I meditate upon these things; give myself wholly to them; that my profiting may appear to all (1 Tim. 4:15, KJV).

I love the law of the Lord; "it is my meditation all the day" (Ps. 119:97, KJV).

The law of the Lord is my delight, and in His law I meditate day and night (Ps. 1:2).

I shall be made to understand the way of the Lord's precepts, so I shall meditate on His wonderful works (Ps. 119:27, NKJV).

I will lift my hands up to the Lord's commandments, which I love, and will meditate on His statutes (Ps. 119:48).

A book of remembrance will be written for me, who fears the Lord and meditates on His name (Mal. 3:16, NKJV).

I will meditate on the Book of the Law day and night (Josh. 1:8).

CHAPTER 6

MERCY AND TRUTH–THE KEYS TO FAVOR WITH GOD AND MAN

> Do not let mercy and truth forsake you; bind them
> around your neck, write them on the tablet of your
> heart, so you will find favor and good understanding
> in the sight of God and man.
>
> —PROVERBS 3:3–4

PROVERBS 3:3–4 TELLS us one of the ways to attract the favor of God is to walk in mercy and truth.

Mercy is the Hebrew word *checed*, which means "kindness, by implication (towards God) piety."[1] It also means favor. In other words, as you show favor to others, you will reap favor. This is simply the law of sowing and reaping. As you are kind to others, showing them mercy and compassion, you will receive favor. To be compassionate is to be concerned about and help others.

Selfish people don't walk in favor. Hardness of heart will stop the flow of God's favor. Those who shut up their bowels of compassion can't expect to walk in God's favor (1 John 3:17).

Psalm 112 describes the kind of person who walks in the favor of the Lord.

> He is gracious [charismatic], and full of compassion [merciful], and righteous [just]. A good man sheweth favour and lendeth,...He hath dispersed [scattered], he hath given to the poor [needy].
> —PSALM 112:4–5, 9, KJV

This person has pity on the poor and gives. He is merciful and compassionate. He sows mercy and reaps favor. Through the law of sowing and reaping, favor is multiplied unto him, because God favors those who favor others.

I've seen people in church who are hard, critical, and judgmental. They have no compassion. They don't forgive or help others. Mercy is at the heart of ministry because you must have compassion for people who are hurting.

Jesus was merciful. He healed the sick, opened blind eyes, and unstopped deaf ears. He stopped and healed those the religious people walked by. He even had mercy on the crowds that followed Him. When they were hungry, He multiplied the fish and loaves to feed them.

Merciful people see the needs of other people. They reach out and help those in need. If you have mercy on people, you will see God's favor come on your life. You may not get a thank-you, but your reward will be the favor of God. God will bless you.

Proverbs 3:3 says, "Do not let mercy *and truth* forsake

you" (emphasis added). Truth is the Hebrew word *emeth*, meaning stability, certainty, truth, and trustworthiness.[2] To be trustworthy means to be reliable. Are you a reliable person? Can people count on you to do what you say? Is your word your bond? These are the questions you need to ask yourself. If you want favor with God and man, you must be trustworthy. You must be faithful. To be faithful means to be worthy of trust or belief.

I've always wanted to be a person of integrity. When people look at me, I want them to know they can count on me to keep my word, that I'll do what I say I will. God honors faithful people. He loves those who love truth. He loves people of integrity.

Consider Daniel. He was "a man greatly beloved" (Dan. 10:11) and had favor with God and man.

> Now God had brought Daniel into favour and tender love with the prince of the eunuchs.
>
> —DANIEL 1:9, KJV

> Then the presidents and princes sought to find occasion against Daniel concerning the kingdom; but they could find none occasion nor fault; forasmuch as he was faithful [trustworthy].
>
> —DANIEL 6:4, KJV

Notice that Daniel was a faithful man. This was a key to Daniel receiving so much favor.

The same was true of Joseph. The Bible says, "Joseph found grace [favor] in his sight" (Gen. 39:4, KJV). He was trustworthy. He would not sin with his master's wife because he was faithful. He knew his master trusted him with everything in his house. He did not sin with Potiphar's wife although she pressed him daily.

If you have not been trustworthy, then repent and begin to keep your word. Become faithful to the house of God. Become a faithful employee. Get to work on time. Be trustworthy on the job. Be trustworthy in all your relationships. Be faithful to your spouse. Make the necessary changes, and watch God's favor begin to flow.

Operate in mercy and truth. Heal the sick. Cast out devils. Feed the hungry. Clothe the naked. These are all mercy ministries.

Preach the truth. Teach the truth. Don't compromise when it comes to the Word of God. God's Word is truth (John 17:17). Be a doer of the Word! Stand on the Word! Defend the truth!

Be truthful. Don't lie. Don't live a hypocritical lifestyle. These things will cut the flow of favor from your life. Don't follow false teaching. Stay with the truth. Follow sound doctrine.

Live a life that is honest before God and man (2 Cor. 8:21). Honesty will cause God's favor to come upon you. God loves honesty. Honesty is truthfulness and sincerity.

> Grace [favor] be with all them that love the Lord
> Jesus Christ in sincerity. Amen.
> —Ephesians 6:24, kjv

Favor is released to those who are sincere in their walk with God. Sincere means genuine with no hypocrisy or pretense. Are you sincere in your walk with God?

If you will walk in mercy and truth, you can expect favor to come into your life.

PRAYERS FOR A HEART OF MERCY AND TRUTH

I take pains to do what is right in the eyes of God and man (2 Cor. 8:21, niv).

I study to show myself "approved by God, a workman who need not be ashamed, rightly dividing the word of truth" (2 Tim. 2:15).

I have put off the old nature and its practices (Col. 3:9).

I speak the truth in Christ and lie not (Rom. 9:1).

I speak truth in love (Eph. 4:15).

I am not ashamed of the gospel; I do not compromise the truth (Rom. 1:16).

I don't rejoice in iniquity; I rejoice in the truth (1 Cor. 13:6).

Fill me with truth in the inward parts, and in the hidden part make me to know wisdom (Ps. 51:6).

I will do unto others as I would have others do unto me (Luke 6:31).

I speak the truth to others; I judge with truth so I will have peace in my gates (Zech. 8:16).

I put away lying and speak truth with my neighbor (Eph. 4:25).

I choose to walk uprightly, do what is righteous, and speak truth from my heart so I can abide in Your tabernacle and dwell in Your holy hill (Ps. 15:1–2).

"My mouth will speak truth, and wickedness is an abomination to my lips" (Prov. 8:7).

My words express the uprightness of my heart, and my lips speak knowledge sincerely (Job 33:3, AMP).

I will not let love and faithfulness leave me; I bind them around my neck, write them on the tablet of my heart that I may win favor and a good name in the sight of God and man (Prov. 3:3–4, NIV).

Like Moses, I will be a faithful servant in God's house (Heb. 3:5).

I fear the Lord, and serve You in sincerity and in truth (Josh. 24:14, KJV).

"Lead me in thy truth, and teach me: for thou art the God of my salvation; on thee do I wait all the day" (Ps. 25:5, KJV).

I will not hide Your righteousness within my heart; I will declare Your faithfulness and salvation. I will not conceal

Your loving-kindness and truth from the great congregation (Ps. 40:10).

May Your "lovingkindness and truth continually preserve me" (Ps. 40:11, KJV).

Let Your light and truth lead me (Ps. 43:3).

"Teach me thy way, O LORD; I will walk in thy truth: unite my heart to fear thy name" (Ps. 86:11, KJV).

Your truth is my shield and buckler (Ps. 91:4, KJV).

"I have chosen the way of truth" (Ps. 119:30, KJV).

I "buy the truth, and sell it not; also wisdom, and instruction, and understanding" (Prov. 23:23, KJV).

Truth is in my mouth, and iniquity will not be found on my lips (Mal. 2:6, KJV).

Mercy and truth preserve me (Prov. 20:28).

I am merciful as my Father is merciful (Luke 6:36).

I have compassion on others just as the Lord has had compassion on me (Matt. 18:33).

I am a true worshipper who worships God "in spirit and in truth" (John 4:23, KJV).

The truth makes me free (John 8:32, KJV).

I love others not only in word but also in deed and in truth (1 John 3:18, KJV).

I am gracious and full of compassion. I show favor and lend. I give to the poor (Ps. 112:4–5, 9, kjv).

I execute true justice and show mercy and compassion (Zech. 7:9).

Like Jesus, I am moved with compassion for those in need (Matt. 14:14; 15:32). I pray with compassion. I prophesy with compassion. I preach with compassion.

Like Moses, I am faithful in the things of God (Num. 12:7).

May I be counted as faithful who fears God and not man (Neh. 7:2).

Find my heart faithful before You (Neh. 9:8).

I will abound with blessings because I am faithful (Prov. 28:20).

I speak Your Word faithfully (Jer. 23:28).

Like Daniel, may I be found faithful, with no error or fault found in me (Dan. 6:4).

I will be a good and faithful servant who proves faithful over a few things so I can be trusted with much (Matt. 25:21).

May I be counted faithful (1 Tim. 1:12).

May I be faithful even unto death so I will receive a crown of life (Rev. 2:10).

CHAPTER 7

EXCELLENCE-THE KEY TO UNCOMMON SUCCESS

And for this same reason, and by applying all diligence,
supply with your faith excellence of character, and
with excellence of character, knowledge.

—2 PETER 1:5, LEB

W E MUST BE people of excellence if we want to see
the favor of God in our lives. We should have a
standard of excellence in our character.

Excellent means extraordinary or exceptional. It means
to be outstanding. According to Bible.org, "Excellence is
a powerful word. It implies something that is obtained
by striving; it is an extremely high ideal."[1] Godly success
through excellence, diligence, and wisdom is not common
in our society of compromise and mediocrity. As people
of God, we were made to stand out as lights illuminating
the glory of God.

The Lord does excellent things (Isa. 12:5). Synonyms
for excellent include exceptional, magnificent, superlative.
Excellence speaks of greatness, completeness, highness,
perfection, and the best. God's greatness is excellent, and

His works are excellent. God's people are called the excellent ones. Do you live up to that name?

> But to the saints that are in the earth, and to the excellent, in whom is all my delight.
>
> —Psalm 16:3, kjv

God will do excellent things for His excellent ones (the saints). This again speaks of those who are in a covenant relationship with Him. We were made in the image of God; therefore, like our Father, we will also do excellent things when we are submitted to Him. Jesus said that we would do greater things than He did (John 14:12).

Believe for excellent things to come to you. Believe that you will do excellent things and see great success and favor in your life. Our God is excellent and will manifest His excellence in your life.

Consider the Ant

> Go to the ant, thou sluggard; consider her ways, and be wise.
>
> —Proverbs 6:6, kjv

The ant is a good example of what characterizes this kind of diligence that leads to life and godliness (2 Pet. 1:3). Ants work tirelessly to gather food in summer for the winter. The ant is the opposite of the sluggard (sloth). The ant does not have an aversion to work. The ant is industrious.

Industrious means working energetically and devotedly; hard-working; diligent.

- The ant is persistent; whether building a nest or gathering food, it sticks with a job until it's done. Do you always stick to a job until it is done and done right?
- It knows its job and does it, working quietly and diligently until the work is done. Do you work without whining or complaining? Do you do your job quietly?
- It doesn't need another ant watching to be sure it completes the task. Can you do a job without someone checking on you or reviewing your work to be sure it is being done and well?
- It is cooperative, working with others to get big jobs done.[2]

The ant is diligent. Diligence is constant and earnest effort to accomplish what is undertaken; it is persistent exertion of body or mind.

Diligence promotes prosperity (riches, plenty) and leads to success.

> He becometh poor that dealeth with a slack hand:
> but the hand of the diligent maketh rich.
> —PROVERBS 10:4, KJV

The thoughts of the diligent tend only to plenteousness; but of every one that is hasty only to want.

—PROVERBS 21:5, KJV

Diligence will put you in a place of authority; it is a key to promotion.

The hand of the diligent shall bear rule: but the slothful shall be under tribute.

—PROVERBS 12:24, KJV

Seest thou a man diligent in his business? he shall stand before kings; he shall not stand before mean men.

—PROVERBS 22:29, KJV

If you will be wise and diligent like the ant, you will see excellence manifest in your life, and you will walk in the favor of God.

PRAYERS OF THE DILIGENT

Father, Your Word says, "The hand of the diligent will rule" (Prov. 12:24). I am diligent, not lazy, and I will rule.

I am not passive; I take action.

My work will go on diligently and prosper in my hands (Ezra 5:8).

I keep Your precepts diligently (Ps. 119:4).

I diligently seek Your face, and I find You (Prov. 7:15).

I will work diligently for the house of the God of heaven (Ezra 7:23, KJV).

I have diligent hands, and "the hand of the diligent makes rich" (Prov. 10:4).

I have diligent hands, and "the hand of the diligent will rule" (Prov. 12:24).

I am diligent, and my plans lead surely to plenty, not poverty (Prov. 21:5).

I diligently present myself "approved to God, a worker who does not need to be ashamed, rightly dividing the word of truth" (2 Tim. 2:15, NKJV).

PRAYERS FOR ENLARGEMENT AND INCREASE

I break any limitations and restrictions placed on my life by evil spirits, in the name of Jesus.

"Bless me indeed, and enlarge my coast." Let Your hand be with me, and keep me from evil (1 Chron. 4:10, KJV).

Cast out my enemies and enlarge my borders (Exod. 34:24).

Enlarge my steps so I can receive Your wealth and prosperity (Isa. 60:5–9).

I receive deliverance and enlargement for my life (Est. 4:14, KJV).

The Lord shall increase me more and more, me and my children (Ps. 115:14).

Let Your kingdom and government increase in my life (Isa. 9:7).

Let me increase in the knowledge of God (Col. 1:10).

O Lord, bless me and increase me (Isa. 51:2, KJV).

Let me increase exceedingly (Gen. 30:43, KJV).

Let me increase with the increase of God (Col. 2:19, KJV).

Let me increase and abound in love (1 Thess. 3:12).

Increase my greatness, and comfort me on every side (Ps. 71:21).

Let me increase in wisdom and stature (Luke 2:52).

Let me increase in strength and confound the adversaries (Acts 9:22).

Let Your grace and favor increase in my life.

Let the years of my life be increased (Prov. 9:11).

Let the Word of God increase in my life (Acts 6:7, KJV).

Let my giving and tithes increase (Deut. 14:22).

CHAPTER 8

PRAYER—THE BOLDNESS TO ASK

> This is the confidence that we have in Him, that if we
> ask anything according to His will, He hears us. So
> if we know that He hears whatever we ask, we know
> that we have whatever we asked of Him.
>
> —1 JOHN 5:14–15

As SIMPLE AS it may seem, a critical key to unlocking the favor of God is to just ask for it. Asking for what we need or want from God is a foundational principle of our relationship with Him as king and ruler over all. He has made Himself available to hear our request. Matthew 7:7–11 (KJV) makes that clear:

> Ask, and it shall be given you; seek, and ye shall
> find; knock, and it shall be opened unto you:
> for every one that asketh receiveth; and he that
> seeketh findeth; and to him that knocketh it shall
> be opened. Or what man is there of you, whom
> if his son ask bread, will he give him a stone? Or
> if he ask a fish, will he give him a serpent? If ye
> then, being evil, know how to give good gifts unto
> your children, how much more shall your Father

which is in heaven give good things to them that ask him?

We see throughout Scripture that God's covenant leaders understood this aspect of mankind's relationship to God and took advantage of it when they came into His presence. You can do the same.

JABEZ—OH, THAT THOU WOULD BLESS ME

The story of Jabez is only two verses (1 Chron. 4:9–10), but it is a powerful reminder of the effectiveness of fervent prayer. The Bible says that Jabez was an honorable man, more honorable than his brothers. Being honorable and having a pure heart before God always play a part in how God answers our prayers. It's not about being perfect, but it is about being holy.

The story of Jabez goes on to reveal that he called on the God of Israel, asking for a blessing, and God granted his request. Jabez's prayer wasn't long and elaborate. He didn't recite the Torah and use lofty words. He simply went before God and said, "'Oh, that You would bless me indeed, and enlarge my territory, that Your hand would be with me, and that You would keep me from evil, that I may not cause pain!' So God granted him what he requested" (v. 10, NKJV). He asked and God gave it to him. Simple.

This teaches us that we can ask God to bless us and that He will grant our request. Jabez asked for God to bless

Him, and He did. God is the source of blessing, and it is the nature of God to be good to His creation. The psalmist says, "The LORD is good, His mercy is everlasting" (Ps. 100:5, NKJV). A revelation of God's goodness will increase our faith for Him to release His blessings and fulfill His promises.

JACOB—I WILL NOT LET GO UNLESS YOU BLESS ME

> Then Jacob was left alone; and a Man wrestled with him until the breaking of day. Now when He saw that He did not prevail against him, He touched the socket of his hip; and the socket of Jacob's hip was out of joint as He wrestled with him. And He said, "Let Me go, for the day breaks." But he said, "I will not let You go unless You bless me!"
>
> —GENESIS 32:24–26, NKJV

This event in Jacob's life came after a long battle for the woman of his dreams. He had diligently worked a total of fourteen years for his wife Rachel. He had hope and expectation behind his efforts. Many of us pray once and immediately get angry with God when He doesn't give us what we prayed for. Jacob didn't do that; he set eyes on his blessing and wouldn't let go until he had it.

But here in Genesis 32, we see Jacob once again in the

midst of a battle, but this time he isn't contending with flesh and blood. He is contending with the supernatural. Jacob had been taught by his forefathers, Abraham and Isaac, about the power and provision of the one true God. He knew that as he came in contact with Him he had an open invitation to request a blessing. And a blessing is what he got.

> So He said to him, "What is your name?" And he said, "Jacob." And He said, "Your name shall no longer be called Jacob, but Israel; for you have struggled with God and with men, and have prevailed." Then Jacob asked, saying, "Tell me Your name, I pray." And He said, "Why is it that you ask about My name?" And He blessed him there. So Jacob called the name of the place Peniel: "For I have seen God face to face, and my life is preserved."
>
> —GENESIS 32:27–30, NKJV

Not only did Jacob come face to face with God, but because he asked, he was also blessed with a new name, purpose, future, and destiny. His whole identity was changed. Jacob experienced what is called a bonanza or a "suddenly" of God. He was instantly taken from being second after Esau, having no inheritance of his own, to being blessed spiritually with an eternal birthright full of the riches of the kingdom of God.

That is what God wants to do for you when you come to Him for a blessing. He wants to give you more than what you ask for because He is good and because He knows how to give good gifts to His children. What you ask Him for is only the start of what He wants to do in your life.

MOSES—PLEASE, SHOW ME YOUR GLORY

Moses longed to see the glory of the Lord. He wanted to dwell in the shadow of the Almighty. He sought hard after God, and God knew him intimately: "For you have found grace in My sight, and I know you by name" (Exod. 33:17, NKJV). So when Moses asked to see the glory of God, he didn't have to make a case for how close he and God were. God knew him by name. Does God know you by name?

We read about the exchange between Moses and God in Exodus 33:17–23. The Lord granted Moses' request because Moses had found favor in His sight, and He caused His goodness to pass before Moses. Goodness is the Hebrew word *ṭûḇ*, meaning goods, good things, goodness, property, fairness, beauty, joy, and prosperity.[1]

The Lord is abundant in goodness and eager to give good gifts to His children. God has laid up His goodness (favor) for us. If we know Him and He knows us, all we have to do is ask Him for it. His blessings and favor are for His children.

Oh how great is thy goodness, which thou hast laid up for them that fear thee; which thou hast wrought for them that trust in thee before the sons of men!

—Psalm 31:19, kjv

We have not because we ask not, so ask the Lord for favor (Jas. 4:2). Ask for favor on the job. Ask for favor in your ministry. Ask God for favor over your business and your family relationships. God delights in giving favor. Ask for God's favor in any area of lack in your life.

Prayers for Blessing and Favor

Lord, bless me and keep me. Make Your face to shine upon me, and be gracious unto me. Lord, lift up Your countenance upon me and give me peace (Num. 6:24–26).

Make me as Ephraim and Manasseh (Gen. 48:20).

Let me be satisfied with favor and filled with Your blessing (Deut. 33:23).

Lord, command Your blessing upon my life.

Give me revelation, and let me be blessed (Matt. 16:17).

I am the seed of Abraham through Jesus Christ, and I receive the blessing of Abraham. Lord, in blessing, bless me, and in multiplying, multiply me as the stars of heaven and as the sand of the seashore (Gen. 22:17).

Let Your "showers of blessing" be upon my life (Ezek. 34:26).

Turn every curse sent my way into a blessing (Neh. 13:2).

Let Your blessing make me rich (Prov. 10:22).

Let all nations call me blessed (Mal. 3:12).

Let all generations call me blessed (Luke 1:48).

I live in the kingdom of the blessed (Mark 11:10).

My sins are forgiven, and I am blessed (Rom. 4.7).

Lord, You daily load me with benefits (Ps. 68:19).

I am chosen by God, and I am blessed (Ps. 65:4).

My seed is blessed (Ps. 37:26, KJV).

Let me inherit the land (Ps. 37:22, NIV).

I am a part of a holy nation, and I am blessed (Ps. 33:12).

Lord, bless my latter end more than my beginning (Job 42:12).

Lord, let Your presence bless my life (2 Sam. 6:11).

I drink the cup of blessing (1 Cor. 10:16).

Lord, bless me, and cause Your face to shine upon me, that Your way may be known upon the earth and Your saving health among all nations. Let my land yield increase, and let the ends of the earth fear You (Ps. 67).

I know You favor me because my enemies do not triumph over me (Ps. 41:11).

Lord, be favorable unto my land (Ps. 85:1).

Lord, grant me life and favor (Job 10:12, KJV).

In Your favor, Lord, make my mountain stand strong (Ps. 30:7, KJV).

Lord, I entreat Your favor (Ps. 45:12).

Let Your favor cause my horn to be exalted (Ps. 89:17).

Lord, this is my set time for favor (Ps. 102:13).

Remember me, O Lord, with the favor that You bring unto Your children, and visit me with Your salvation (Ps. 106:4, KJV).

Lord, I entreat Your favor with my whole heart (Ps. 119:58, KJV).

Let Your favor be upon my life "as a cloud of the latter rain" (Prov. 16:15, KJV).

Let Your beauty be upon my life and let me be well favored (Gen. 29:17, KJV).

I am highly favored (Luke 1:28).

Lord, let me receive extraordinary favor.

Let me be well favored (Gen. 39:6, KJV).

Lord, show me mercy and give me favor (Gen. 39:21).

Give me favor in the sight of the world (Exod. 12:36).

Let me be satisfied with your favor like Naphtali (Deut. 33:23).

Let me have favor with You, Lord, and with men (1 Sam. 2:26).

Let me have favor with the king (1 Sam. 16:22).

Let me have great favor in the sight of the king (1 Kings 11:19, KJV).

Let me find favor like Esther (Est. 2:17).

"Thou hast granted me life and favour, and Thy visitation hath preserved my spirit" (Job 10:12, KJV).

I pray unto You, Lord, grant me favor (Job 33:26).

Bless me and surround me "with favor like a shield" (Ps. 5:12).

In Your favor is life (Ps. 30:5).

Because of Your favor, the enemy will not triumph over me (Ps. 41:11).

Through Your favor, I am brought back from captivity (Ps. 85:1).

Let my horn be exalted through Your favor (Ps. 89:17).

Let Your favor be upon my life as the dew upon the grass (Prov. 19:12).

I choose Your "loving favor rather than gold and silver" (Prov. 22:1).

Let me be highly favored (Luke 1:28).

Show me Your marvelous loving-kindness (Ps. 17:7).

Remember Your mercy and loving-kindness in my life (Ps. 25:6).

"Your lovingkindness is before my eyes" (Ps. 26:3).

I receive Your excellent loving-kindness (Ps. 36:7).

Continue Your loving-kindness in my life (Ps. 36:10, KJV).

Let Your loving-kindness and Your truth continually preserve me (Ps. 40:11, KJV).

Command Your loving-kindness in the daytime (Ps. 42:8, KJV).

Your "lovingkindness is good: turn unto me according to the multitude of Thy tender mercies" (Ps. 69:16, KJV).

"Quicken me after Thy lovingkindness" (Ps. 119:88, KJV).

Hear my voice according to Your loving-kindness (Ps. 119:149, KJV).

Lord, You are the source of my blessing.

Lord, I choose blessing by walking in Your covenant.

Lord, command Your blessing upon my life.

Lord, You are the father of lights, and You give good gifts. Release Your gifts into my life (Jas. 1:17).

Lord, I trust in You, and I receive Your blessing.

Lord, I ask and I receive Your blessing (Matt. 7:7).

Lord, I seek and find Your blessing (Matt. 7:7).

Lord, I knock, and the door of blessing is opened to me (Luke 11:9).

Lord, I ask for blessings in the name of Jesus, and I believe You give them to me.

Lord, You are a God who blesses and rewards those who diligently seek after You (Heb. 11).

Lord, You are a fountain of (life) blessing.

Lord, You are a tree of (life) blessing.

Lord, release Your river of blessing into my life.

Lord, rain upon my life, and pour out Your blessing over me.

Lord, release the blessing of heaven and the blessing of the deep into my life (Gen. 49:25, KJV).

Lord, release the blessing of the breast and the womb into my life (Gen. 49:25, KJV).

Let the blessing of Abraham come on my life (Gal. 3:13–14).

Let me be blessed with authority (Gen. 49:10).

Let me be a fruitful bough whose branches run over the wall (Gen. 49:22).

Lord, bless my substance and the work of my hands (Deut. 33:11).

Lord, bless my land, and let the dew of heaven be upon me (Deut. 33:13).

Lord, enlarge me like Gad (Deut. 33:20).

Lord, let me be satisfied with favor, and let me be full of Your blessing like Naphtali (Deut. 33:23).

Lord, let me dwell in safety, and cover me like Benjamin (Deut. 33:12).

Let me reap a hundredfold like Isaac (Gen. 26:12).

Let me be blessed like Jacob (Gen. 28:1).

Lord, Jabez asked You to bless him, and You did. Bless me like Jabez (1 Chron. 4:10).

Lord, bless me and make me fruitful like Ishmael (Gen. 17:20).

Lord, bless me with a blessing that cannot be reversed (Num. 23:20).

Let my basket and store be blessed (Deut. 28:5, KJV).

Lord, bless my beginning and my latter end like Job's (Job 42:12).

Lord, bless me with wisdom like Solomon.

Lord, give me favor like Nehemiah to finish the assignment You have given me (Neh. 2:5).

Lord, bless me to inherit my territory like Caleb and Joshua (Num. 32:12).

Lord, let me win every battle like David.

PRAYERS FOR BONANZAS AND BREAKTHROUGHS

Lord, let my desire come, and let it be "a tree of life" (Prov. 13:12).

Let understanding be "a wellspring of life" for me (Prov. 16:22).

Lord, let Your fear give me life (blessing); let me be satisfied, and let me not be visited with evil (Prov. 19:23, KJV).

Lord, let humility and the fear of You bring riches, life (blessing), and honor (Prov. 22:4).

I will live and not die, and will declare the work of the Lord (Ps. 118:17).

Lord, show me "the path of life; in Your presence is fullness of joy; at Your right hand there are pleasures for evermore" (Ps. 16:11).

Lord, give me life and length of days (Ps. 21:4).

Lord, give me Your favor, for in Your favor is life (Ps. 30:5).

"For with You is the fountain of life; in Your light we see light" (Ps. 36:9).

Let Your wisdom be "a tree of life" to me (Prov. 3:18).

Let Your words be life to my soul and grace to my neck (Prov. 3:22).

I will hold fast to instruction because it is my life (Prov. 4:13).

I have found wisdom, I have found life, and I obtain Your favor (Prov. 8:35).

Lord, You have redeemed my life from destruction. You crown me with loving-kindness and tender mercies (Ps. 103:4).

Let me enjoy the blessing of fruitfulness and multiplication (Gen. 1:22).

Let Your blessing come upon my family (Gen. 12:3).

I am blessed through Christ, the seed of Abraham (Gen. 22:18).

Let me be blessed greatly (Gen. 24:35).

Let those connected to me be blessed (Gen. 30:27).

Let me receive blessed advice (1 Sam. 25:33).

I walk not in the counsel of the ungodly, I stand not in the way of sinners, and I sit not in the seat of the scornful, but I delight in the law of the Lord, and I am blessed (Ps. 1, KJV).

Bless me, Lord, for I put my trust in You (Ps. 2:12, KJV).

Lord, I receive Your blessing for my transgression is forgiven and my sin is covered (Ps. 32:1).

Lord, bless me; I renounce and turn away from all guile, and iniquity is not imputed to me (Ps. 32:2).

Lord, bless me; You are my trust. I respect not the proud nor such as turn aside to lies (Ps. 40:4, KJV).

Lord, bless me; I consider the poor. Deliver me in the time of trouble, preserve me, and keep me alive. Bless me upon the earth and deliver me not unto the will of my enemies (Ps. 41:1–2).

Lord, bless me for You have chosen me and caused me to approach unto You and dwell in Your courts, that I might be satisfied with the goodness of Your house (Ps. 65:4).

Lord, daily load me with benefits (Ps. 68:19).

Lord, bless me as I dwell in Your house and continue to praise You (Ps. 84:4).

Bless me, Lord; my strength is in You (Ps. 84:5).

Bless me, Lord, and let the light of Your countenance shine on me; I know the joyful sound (Ps. 89:15).

Let me be blessed by Your correction, and teach me out of Your Word (Ps. 94:12).

Bless me, Lord, and let me keep Your judgments and "do righteousness at all times" (Ps. 106:3).

Bless me, Lord, for I fear You and delight greatly in Your commandments (Ps. 112:1).

Bless me, Lord; I fear You and walk in Your ways (Ps. 128:1).

Bless me, Lord; I receive wisdom, watching daily at wisdom's gates, waiting at the posts of wisdom's doors (Prov. 8:34, KJV).

Lord, I have a bountiful (generous) eye; bless me (Prov. 22:9).

Bless me, Lord; I wait on You (Isa. 30:18, KJV).

I "sow beside all waters"; bless me, Lord (Isa. 32:20).

Bless me, Lord; I will "not labor in vain nor bring forth children for trouble" (Isa. 65:23).

Bless me, Lord. I trust in You, and my hope is in You (Jer. 17:7).

Let all nations call me blessed, and let me be a delightful land (Mal. 3:12).

Anoint me for breakthrough (Isa. 61).

Let me experience breakthroughs in every area of my life.

Let me break through all limitations and obstacles.

I will expand my tent, lengthen my cords, and strengthen my stakes, because I will experience breakthrough (Isa. 54:2, KJV).

The Lord my "breaker" goes before me (Mic. 2:13, KJV).

Let me break through in my finances.

Let me break through in relationships.

Let me break through in my health with healing.

Let me break through in my ministry.

Let me break through in my city.

Let me break through in my emotions.

Let me break through in my praise.

Let me break through in my prayer life.

Let me break through in my worship.

Let me break through in my revelation.

Let me break through in my career.

Let me break through in my giving.

Let me experience bonanzas in my life.

Let me experience Your "suddenlies," Lord.

Do "a quick work" in my life (Rom. 9:28).

Let me experience great increase in a short period of time.

I believe in and confess *bonanzas* for my life.

Let me find the vein of prosperity and experience bonanzas.

CHAPTER 9

ENTER GOD'S BEST

If you are willing and obedient, you shall eat the good of the land.

—ISAIAH 1:19

O NE TUESDAY NIGHT during a service at the church I pastor in Chicago, I prophesied about moving into a good land. After delivering that word, I did a Scripture word study regarding "the land"—the land of Canaan, the Promised Land, inheriting the land, and the good land.

I discovered that the good land is a picture of the kingdom and living in the promises of God. The good land is God's country. It is a place where goodness, abundance, prosperity, excellence, refreshing, beauty, nourishment, blessing, satisfaction, plenty, and glory are ways of life. It is the land of the finest, best, and choicest of meat and grain. It is a place where we are nourished, shielded, and safe. We receive abundant harvests, and all our works are fruitful in the good land. It is a place where becoming "fat and large" is a spiritual picture of prosperity, wealth, and the anointing.

The good land I speak of is not a physical place but a

spiritual representation of what was purchased for us by the finished work of Jesus at the cross. It is a metaphor for our spiritual inheritance in Christ and the favor we have as a result. So now because of Christ the saints of God dwell in this land and possess it by faith.

Through the Old Testament types and shadows, we see how the people of Israel moved from a land of not enough (Egypt) to a land of just enough (the wilderness) to a land of more than enough—Canaan, the Promised Land. God is doing this for us too. He has brought us out of the world— Egypt, the land of not enough—through the wilderness, where our needs are just being met, and now God wants to bring us into a land of more than enough.

God wants to be your *El Shaddai*, the God of more than enough. He will anoint your head with oil until your cup overflows and runs over. The land of promise is a land of overflow, open heaven, downpour, and abundance; a land where goodness and mercy will follow you all the days of your life (Ps. 23:6). This is what God intends for you—His best. It is God's plan for you to come out of the wilderness and cross over into the land of favor and blessing, the place of His best.

THE BEST OF THE BEST

You must get it in your spirit that the good land is God's best, and it is God's will for you to have it. Many of us have been taught that we shouldn't expect or want the best, that we shouldn't think of ourselves worthy enough to be the best or go after it. This is not God's plan for you. He delights in the prosperity of His servants (Ps. 35:27, KJV).

God, of course, is the best. He is the highest and most excellent. Not only is He the best, but He also gives the best. God wants you to have the best.

I prophesied one Sunday that we would enter a season of God's best, which goes hand in hand with the revelation of our entering into a good land. The verse the Lord gave me concerning this was Psalm 147:14: "He maketh peace in thy borders, and filleth thee with the finest of the wheat" (KJV). The best is the finest. The New Life Version translates this verse, "He makes peace within your walls. He fills you with the best grain."

As I conducted a word study for the word *best*, I discovered synonyms such as "finest, greatest, top, foremost, leading, preeminent, premier, prime, first, chief, principal, supreme, of the highest quality, superlative, par excellence, unrivaled, second to none, without equal…peerless, matchless…optimal…ideal…highest, record breaking."[1]

Best in Hebrew is *heleb* or *cheleb*. It comes "from an unused root meaning to be fat; fat, whether literally or figuratively; hence, the richest or choice part: —best, fat(-ness), finest, grease, marrow"; "choicest, best part, abundance (of products of the land)."[2] In other words, God wants to give us the best of the best.

I challenge you to believe and confess that you will enjoy the finest. Believe for God's best in your life. Believe for the best doors, the best relationships, the best finances, the best promotions, the best blessings, the best favor, the best increase, the best breakthroughs, the best insight, the best vision, the best praise, the best worship, the best harvest, the best land, and the best ideas.

Because of Jesus' sacrifice we can live as though we believe Jesus gives us the best. He even made a statement about His giving the best in His first public miracle, when He turned water into wine at the wedding at Cana.

> And said to him, "People always serve the best wine first. Later, when the guests are drunk, they serve the cheaper wine. But you have saved the best wine until now."
>
> —JOHN 2:10, ERV

A few verses earlier we see where Mary, Jesus' mother, told Jesus that they had run out of wine. Jesus answered, "Why do you involve me? ...My hour has not yet come" (John 2:4, NIV). It seems that Mary ignored Him and told the servants to do whatever He told them to do. The Bible says, "They did so" (v. 8, NIV). And here we see that one way to begin to walk in God's best is to do what He says to do—be obedient.

Jesus can turn your water into wine. He can transform what is normal into the best. This can happen if you do what He says.

TAKE INVENTORY

You may be wondering why you are not enjoying God's best, and sometimes, if you're honest, you put it on God, saying, "Maybe it's not the will of God for me to have it." Let me assure you: it is the will of God for you to live in the good land, but it is also the will of God for you to be willing and obedient so that you can eat the good of the land (Isa. 1:19–20).

If you are a believer but are not entering into the promises of God after years and years of confession, praying, shouting, and dancing, you need to take an inventory of your life. Ask yourself:

- Is there any pride in my life?
- Do I get angry when corrected?
- Is there an area in my life where I am not obeying God?
- Do I talk about my supervisors or church leadership?
- Do I hate my bosses or the leaders in my church?
- Do I criticize authority in various areas of my life?
- Do I always have a problem with leadership?
- Do I run from church to church?

- Am I double-minded?
- Do I operate in rejection and rebellion?

These are things that can prevent you from entering into the fullness of God's promises. God desires that you be free. He wants the best for you. And He absolutely wants you to be able to enjoy the good land. But He doesn't bless mess. You are called to adhere to God's standard of holiness and righteousness as you grow in Christ. Let the Spirit of God lead you into all truth, which sets you free.

RECEIVING GOD'S BEST

When it comes to receiving God's best, the first thing we should set our minds toward is to not accept less than God's best. The next thing is to give back to God our best, including our best sacrifices and offerings.

> All the best of the oil, and all the best of the wine, and of the wheat, the first fruits of what they will offer unto the LORD, those have I given to you.
> —NUMBERS 18:12

Finally, we must listen to God and walk in His ways, as Psalm 81 instructs.

> Oh that my people had hearkened unto me, and Israel had walked in my ways! I should soon have subdued their enemies, and turned my hand against their adversaries. The haters of the LORD

should have submitted themselves unto him:
but their time should have endured for ever. He
should have fed them also with the finest [best] of
the wheat: and with honey out of the rock should
I have satisfied thee.

—PSALM 81:13–16, KJV

We must listen to and obey the voice of God and
follow His direction if we are to live in His best. In other
words, we must walk in His ways—in love, mercy, truth,
righteousness, forgiveness, holiness, and faith. God will
teach us His ways (Ps. 86:11; 143:8) so we can walk in the
blessing promised in the Book of Deuteronomy:

The LORD shall command the blessing upon thee
in thy storehouses, and in all that thou settest
thine hand unto; and he shall bless thee in the
land which the LORD thy God giveth thee. The
LORD shall establish thee an holy people unto
himself, as he hath sworn unto thee, if thou shalt
keep the commandments of the LORD thy God,
and walk in his ways. And all people of the earth
shall see that thou art called by the name of the
LORD; and they shall be afraid of thee.

—DEUTERONOMY 28:8–10, KJV

When you walk in His ways, God commands His
blessing upon your life. God commands the best for your
life.

Favor will take you to the best place. Though Esther was taken from her home and put into a life she did not want, we can trace God's favor over her life as He provided her with the best place among the other women. She received His best protection and wisdom to bring deliverance to her people. Just as Esther received favor for God's best (Est. 2:15, 17), you can be favored with the best.

> And the maiden pleased him, and she obtained kindness of him; and he speedily gave her her things for purification, with such things as belonged to her, and seven maidens, which were meet to be given her, out of the king's house: and he preferred her and her maids unto the best place of the house of the women.
>
> —ESTHER 2:9, KJV

Esther and her maidens were taken to the best place. They had the best rooms. The Living Bible calls it "the most luxurious apartment."

God wants you to have the best. Appropriate it by faith. Confess the promises of God and expect nothing but the best. Be ready to follow God to the good land, the place of peace, prosperity, enlargement, bounty, beauty, and rest from all your enemies.

GOOD LAND CONFESSIONS

I am willing and obedient, and I will eat the good of the land (Ezra 9:12; Isa. 1:19).

I enter the good land by faith.

The good land is my inheritance in Christ.

I enjoy the blessing and prosperity of the good land. The river of God flows into my life (Ps. 65:9, KJV).

The rain of heaven falls upon my life (Deut. 11:11, KJV). My harvest is plentiful.

I lack nothing in the good land. I drink the milk and eat the honey (Num. 14:8). I am nourished in the good land. I enjoy the sweetness of the Lord. I come to the mountain of God (Exod. 3:1, KJV).

I am a part of Zion.

I live under the rule and reign of God. I enjoy God's goodness in this land.

I am like a cedar of Lebanon (Ps. 104:16; Isa. 14:8, KJV).

The hills drop new wine in my life. I enjoy the fatness of the Lord.

I drink from the fountain of living waters (Jer. 2:13; 17:13).

I enjoy the finest of the wheat (Ps. 147:14).

I enjoy the fruits of the land. There is a good scent in my life. I wash my steps in butter.

The rock pours out rivers of oil for me. I am anointed with fresh oil.

I eat and I am satisfied.

I praise God for His goodness in this land.

The glory of the Lord is upon my life in the good land. I live in a wealthy place.

I live in a large place.

The heavens are open over my life.

The Lord opens unto me His good treasure. I receive an abundance of rain.

I enjoy the new wine of the Spirit. I sit under my own fig tree.

I have my own vineyard. I will lend and not borrow (Deut. 28:12).

I enjoy a continual feast in the good land (Prov. 15:15).

The beauty of the Lord is upon my life. I have beauty for ashes (Isa. 61:3). I walk in the strength and comfort of the Lord. I enter into rest in the good land.

I live in safety in the good land. The dew of heaven is upon my life.

The word from heaven drops upon my life. My life is filled with moisture and sap.

I am a tree of righteousness, the planting of the Lord (Isa. 61:3). I enjoy good things.

There is no famine in my life.

I am Abraham's seed and heir according to the promise (Gal. 3:29).

Through meekness I inherit the land (Matt. 5:5).

CONFESSIONS FOR THE BEST

The best is yet to come.

I will walk into the best.

I release my faith for the best.

My worst days and years are behind me.

I serve the God of the best.

May the Lord command the best for my life.

My God is the best, and He gives me the best.

I live in the land, and I enjoy the best.

I am favored with the best.

My God knows what is best for me.

I will live my best life.

I will live and walk in excellence.

I will pursue and desire what is excellent.

I will approve things that are excellent.

I will have an excellent spirit.

Let excellent glory be on my life.

My God will do excellent things in my life.

Let heaven release the best blessings over my life.

Let my life overflow with the best.

God's ways are the best ways for my life.

God's plans are the best plans for my future.

I will be willing and obedient, and I will eat the best of the land.

God chooses my inheritance and gives me the best.

This will be one of the best years of my life.

I will make the best choices.

My God teaches me to profit and leads me in the way I should go.

My finances will be the best.

I will enjoy God's best.

I will eat the finest of the wheat. I will make the best decisions.

I will walk in the best paths.

I will enjoy fatness and marrow in the house of the Lord.

I will receive the best blessings.

I will give the Lord my best.

I will give Him my best praise and worship.

I will receive the best ministry.

I will give the best offerings.

My thinking will be the best. My speaking will be the best.

I will understand things that are excellent.

I will speak things that are excellent.

I will have the best:

- The best relationships
- The best sleep and rest
- The best peace (shalom)
- The best fellowship
- The best ideas
- The best wisdom
- The best understanding
- The best gifts
- The best breakthroughs
- The best doors

- The best health
- The best vision
- The best hope
- The best desires
- The best motives
- The best plans
- The best insight
- The best discernment
- The best discounts
- The best surprises
- The best increase
- The best promotions
- The best oil (anointing)
- The best wine (move of the Spirit)
- The best help
- The best assignments
- The best alignments
- The best organization
- The best order
- The best timing
- The best gatherings
- The best communication
- The best teaching
- The best preaching
- The best thoughts
- The best music

- The best songs
- The best marriage
- The best inventions
- The best progress
- The best changes
- The best moves
- The best successes
- The best counsel
- The best course of action
- The best harvest
- The best impact
- The best protection
- The best safety
- The best creativity
- The best innovation
- The best investments

FAT AND FLOURISHING CONFESSIONS

I am like a green olive tree in the house of the Lord.

I will be satisfied with marrow and fatness.

I will enjoy the fatness of God's house.

I will be fat and flourishing.

The anointing in my life destroys all yokes.

I am growing large and increasing, and I burst every yoke.

My neck is too large for the yokes of the enemy.

I enjoy the fatness of the kingdom.

I feast on what is fat and good.

God prepares a table before me (Ps. 23:5).

I eat at God's table.

God feeds me and makes me strong.

I am liberal, and I am made fat.

My bones are fat and flourishing.

I break every yoke because of prosperity.

I enjoy abundance and prosperity.

I receive and walk in God's best for my life.

I eat the fat and drink the sweet, and the joy of the Lord is my strength.

God anoints my head with oil, and my cup runs over (Ps. 23:5).

I dwell in the land, and I am fed.

I enjoy the fat of the land.

CHAPTER 10

PRAYERS AND DECREES TO RELEASE THE FAVOR OF GOD

Death and life are in the power of the tongue, and
those who love it will eat its fruit.

—PROVERBS 18:21

CONFESSING THE WORD of God is an important part
of every believer's spiritual life. Christianity is called
the "great confession." Salvation comes from confessing
with the mouth that Jesus Christ is Lord (Rom. 10:9–10).
The mouth is connected to the heart, and the Word of God
released from your mouth will be planted in your heart.
Faith is also released from the mouth. The Bible says, "Out
of the abundance of the heart the mouth speaks" (Matt.
12:34). The mouth can only release what is in the heart.
But faith in the heart that is released through the mouth
can move mountains (Matt. 17:20).

God's Word is powerful. When you pray the Word of
God, it becomes "like a hammer that breaks the rock in
pieces" (Jer. 23:29), bringing victory and the abundant life
Jesus died for us to experience. May the following prayers
and confessions activate your faith and expectancy for

God's best and release His favor and goodness as you walk faithfully before Him.

FAVOR DECREES AND CONFESSIONS

I believe in Jesus. I confess Him as my Lord. I am justified by faith. I have been declared righteous. I am the righteousness of God in Christ. I have been reconciled. I am back in favored status with God.

I am increasing in favor with God and man. I humble myself and receive more favor and grace in my life.

I come boldly to the throne of favor. I obtain mercy and favor in the time of need. I ask You, Lord, for favor.

I am increasing in wisdom, knowledge, and understanding, and I am increasing in favor.

I am a giver, and I enjoy favor. God makes all favor abound in my life, and I have sufficiency in all things.

My gifts make room for me and bring me before great men (Prov. 18:16).

I have favor with influential and powerful people.

Every curse against me is turned into a blessing because of favor.

Favor attracts wealth and riches and brings them into my life.

Favor brings the right people into my life.

Favor causes bills to be decreased and paid off.

Favor causes me to lend and not borrow.

Favor causes me to be enlarged.

Favor causes me to break limitations.

Favor causes me to enjoy the best.

Favor causes me to see what others miss.

Favor causes me to succeed where others fail.

Favor causes people to bless me.

Favor causes people to help and assist me.

Favor enables me to overcome opposition.

Favor expands my borders.

Favor floods my life.

Favor flows out of my life like a river.

Favor follows me wherever I go.

Favor follows me.

Favor gives me bonuses and bonanzas.

Favor gives me discounts and dividends.

Favor gives me gifts and surprises.

Favor gives me multiplied victories.

_____

Favor gives me new opportunities.

_____

Favor gives me second chances.

_____

Favor is multiplied in my life.

_____

Favor is my portion in life.

_____

Favor is poured from heaven upon my life.

_____

Favor lifts me above my enemies.

_____

Favor locates me wherever I go.

_____

Favor makes difficult things easy for me.

_____

Favor places me above and not beneath.

_____

Favor makes me the head and not the tail.

_____

Favor makes my mountain strong.

_____

Favor makes my way prosperous.

_____

Favor makes the impossible possible for me.

_____

Favor opens doors for me.

_____

Favor paves the way for my success.

_____

Favor promotes me.

_____

Favor surrounds me like a shield.

_____

Favor causes me to go where others cannot go.

God causes things to work in my favor.

God has marked me for favor.

God's favor falls on me like rain.

I always increase in favor.

I am a recipient of the King's favor.

I am clothed in favor.

I am covered by the flood of favor.

I am highly favored.

I am impacted by the winds of favor.

I am one of God's favorites.

I am overwhelmed by an avalanche of favor.

I am refreshed by the dew of favor.

I am revived by the breath of favor.

I am rich with favor.

I am soaked in the rain of favor.

I am surrounded by favor.

I ask and receive wisdom and favor.

PRAYERS THAT UNLOCK FAVOR

I associate with those who are favored.

I come to the throne of favor.

I confess and receive a crown of favor.

I confess and receive a free flow of favor.

I confess and receive an abundance of favor.

I confess and receive an anointing for favor.

I confess and receive an avalanche of favor.

I confess and receive extraordinary favor.

I confess and receive favor with influential people.

I confess and receive heaps of favor.

I confess and receive mega favor.

I confess and receive special favor.

I confess and receive the King's favor.

I confess and receive unusual favor.

I confess favor for today and the future.

I draw from the well of favor.

I drink from the fountain of favor.

I enjoy a lifetime of favor.

I enjoy extreme favor.

I enjoy financial favor.

I enjoy new favor.

I go from favor to favor.

I harvest from the field of favor.

I have a banner of favor over my life.

I have a lifetime of favor.

I have an abundance of favor.

I have an angel of favor.

I have an anointing for favor.

I have favor for breakthroughs.

I have favor for health and prosperity.

I have favor for thousands and ten thousands.

I have favor in my city.

I have favor with God and man.

I have financial favor.

I have gifts that bring favor.

I have strong faith for favor.

I have the dew of favor on my life.

I live by the river of favor.

I live in a new season of favor.

I live under a cloud of favor.

I live with unusual favor.

I praise the Lord for favor.

I reap heaps of favor.

I receive a downpour of favor.

I receive favorable reports.

I receive gifts and grants through favor.

I receive the word of favor.

I release my faith for favor.

I sow favor, and I reap a harvest of favor.

I understand favor.

I walk in divine favor.

I walk in extraordinary favor.

I walk in the path of favor.

I walk in the revelation of favor.

I wear the coat of favor.

I wear the crown of favor.

I will never lack favor.

I will sing about favor.

I will walk in mercy and truth, and I will walk in favor.

Let the river of favor flow into my life.

My career is favored.

My cup runs over with favor.

My ideas are favored.

My life overruns with favor.

My projects are favored.

My relationships are favored.

My steps are favored of the Lord.

The glory of God is upon me, and I enjoy His favor.

The wealth of the wicked comes into my hand because of favor.

The winds of favor blow in my life.

This is a set time of favor for my life.

Time and chance work in my favor.

What the enemy meant for evil works in my favor.

Wisdom gives me favor.

LEAP PRAYERS FOR SUDDEN INCREASE AND DRAMATIC ADVANCE

The following prayers are taken from Deuteronomy 32:22; 2 Samuel 6:16; Psalm 18:29; Isaiah 35:6; Luke 1:41; Luke 6:23; Acts 3:8; and Acts 14:10.

I believe this is my appointed time to leap forward, in the name of Jesus.

It is my time to leap.

This is a new season of leaping for me.

I leap past all distractions, in the name of Jesus.

I leap past any people the enemy has set in my way to impede my progress.

Let my steps turn into leaps.

I leap over every wall erected by the enemy.

In the name of Jesus, I leap ahead of anyone or anything that has illegally jumped ahead of me.

I leap like a lion from Bashan like Dan.

I will leap over my enemies like David.

I receive strength to leap out of all sickness and disease. I leap into my destiny and purpose, in the name of Jesus.

With excitement I leap into my future.

I leap from lack to abundance.

I leap from failure to success.

Let every place in my life that is lame leap for joy.

I take a leap of faith and do the impossible.

Let my finances grow by leaps and bounds.

Let my finances leap to a level I have not seen before.

Let wealth and prosperity leap upon my life, in the name of Jesus.

Let my wisdom increase by leaps and bounds.

Let my understanding increase by leaps and bounds.

Let my vision increase by leaps and bounds.

Let favor increase on my life by leaps and bounds.

Let my ministry grow by leaps and bounds.

Let my borders expand by leaps and bounds.

Let me leap and jump to the high places.

In the name of Jesus, let me catch up in any place I have fallen behind.

Let restoration come from anything stolen by the enemy from my life.

Let my revelation increase by leaps and bounds.

I will not be afraid to take a leap of faith at the word of the Lord.

I will leap upon the enemy and overwhelm him, in the name of Jesus.

I will leap and rejoice at the goodness of the Lord.

The Lord has given me leaping for sadness and joy for mourning.

I leap from a low place to a high place.

Let extra favor and blessing be added to my life, in the name of Jesus.

Let this year be a year of uncommon favor and blessing in my life.

Let me receive uncommon miracles and breakthroughs, in the name of Jesus.

Let me leap as a hart for joy.

I will leap into new places naturally and spiritually.

I will leap into new heights and levels.

I will leap above problems and setbacks, in the name of Jesus.

I will leap over all the traps and snares of the wicked one.

I break all chains and weights from my feet that would prevent me from leaping.

I lay aside every weight and burden that would prevent me from leaping.

I lay aside all doubt and unbelief that would keep me from leaping.

I leap from my past into my future.

I will not be afraid to leap forward with boldness and confidence.

I will leap, for my God is with me.

My God encourages me and causes me to leap forward.

Let the kingdom advance in my city by leaps and bounds.

Let my timing and purpose be realigned this year, in the name of Jesus.

The way is opened for me, and I will leap into it.

I will join myself with other believers who are leaping forward.

Let the churches in my region leap forward. Let our praise and worship leap to another level.

Let my prayer life leap forward.

Let our preaching and teaching leap to another level.

I will leap forward in my giving.

Let my creativity leap to another level.

Let my faith take a quantum leap.

Let my love take a quantum leap.

Let my family leap forward into destiny.

Let my prophetic level take a quantum leap.

Let deliverance and healing take a quantum leap in my city, in the name of Jesus.

I will leap through fasting and prayer.

Let the blessings of the Lord overtake me and leap upon me, in the name of Jesus.

PRAYERS FOR YOUR CHILDREN TO WALK IN GOD'S FAVOR

Father, I thank You for Your favor. I believe in the power of favor.

I humble myself and ask for Your favor on my children. They need Your favor in every area of their lives.

I believe my children are increasing in favor. I declare that they desire to walk in higher levels of favor. They receive an abundance of favor, and they reign in life through Your favor. They receive great favor.

As my children grow in the knowledge of You and the Lord

Jesus Christ, I believe favor is multiplied unto them. They are givers. As they give, Your favor abounds toward them. I declare that they are merciful and trustworthy. They have favor with God and man.

I believe You will support, endorse, help, make things easier, promote, and honor my children because of Your favor. They will enjoy "favored child" status from their heavenly Father. Your favor surrounds my children as a shield.

Your favor overflows in my children's lives. Thank You, Father, for Your favor on them.

I praise You and give You glory for Your favor on my children's lives.

Lord, You have granted my children life and favor.

I thank You for favor coming upon my children's lives.

I believe that new life and new favor have been ordained for my children.

Today my children receive new life and new favor.

I believe favor is a gift of heaven.

My children receive the gift of life—the gift of eternal life.

My children receive the gift of favor and the gift of grace upon their lives, in the name of Jesus.

Thank You, Lord, for new grace and new favor, new prosperity and new blessing coming on my children's lives.

My children are the apple of God's eye.

My children are God's favorites.

God favors, loves, and has chosen my children from the foundation of the world to receive His grace and favor.

My children receive extraordinary favor on their lives in the name of Jesus!

Let my children be well favored (Gen. 39:6, KJV).

Lord, show my children mercy and give them favor (Gen. 39:21).

Give my children favor in the sight of the world (Exod. 12:36).

Let my children be satisfied with Your favor like Naphtali (Deut. 33:23).

Let my children have favor with You, Lord, and with men (1 Sam. 2:26).

Let my children have favor with the king (1 Sam. 16:22).

Let my children have great favor in the sight of the king (1 Kings 11:19).

Let my children find favor like Esther (Est. 2:17).

Thou hast granted my children life and favour, and Thy visitation hath preserved their spirits (Job 10:12, KJV).

I pray unto You, Lord, grant my children favor (Job 33:26).

Bless my children and surround them with favor like a shield (Ps. 5:12).

Make my children's mountain stand strong by Your favor (Ps. 30:7).

Because of Your favor, the enemy will not triumph over my children (Ps. 41:11).

Through Your favor, my children are brought back from captivity (Ps. 85:1).

Let the horn of my children be exalted through Your favor (Ps. 89:17).

My children's set time of favor has come (Ps. 102:13).

I entreat Your favor on behalf of my children with my whole heart (Ps. 119:58, KJV).

Let Your favor be for my children as a cloud of the latter rain (Prov. 16:15).

Let Your favor be upon my children's lives as the dew upon the grass (Prov. 19:12).

My children choose Your loving favor rather than gold and silver (Prov. 22:1).

Let my children be highly favored (Luke 1:28).

NOTES

CHAPTER 1

1. *Merriam-Webster*, s.v. "reconcile," accessed July 10, 2023, https://www.merriam-webster.com/dictionary/reconcile.

CHAPTER 4

1. Bible Tools, s.v. "*megas*," accessed April 28, 2023, https://www.bibletools.org/index.cfm/fuseaction/Lexicon.show/ID/G3173/megas.htm.
2. *Merriam-Webster*, s.v. "mega," accessed April 28, 2023, https://www.merriam-webster.com/dictionary/mega.
3. *Merriam-Webster*, s.v. "enrich," accessed April 28, 2023, https://www.merriam-webster.com/dictionary/enrich.
4. *Merriam-Webster*, s.v. "rich," accessed April 28, 2023, https://www.merriam-webster.com/dictionary/rich.

CHAPTER 6

1. Blue Letter Bible, s.v. "*checed*," accessed April 18, 2023, https://www.blueletterbible.org/lexicon/h2617/kjv/wlc/0-1/.

2. Bible Tools, s.v. "*emeth*," accessed April 28, 2023, https://www.bibletools.org/index.cfm/fuseaction/ Lexicon.show/ID/H571/emeth.htm.

CHAPTER 7

1. Richard Ostella, "The Excellence of Christian Love (1 Cor. 12:31-13:3)," Bible.org. accessed July 10, 2023, https://bible.org/seriespage/1-excellence- christian-love-1-cor-1231-133.
2. "God Speaks of the Ant in His Word, the Bible," Answers in Genesis, March 23, 2010, https:// answersingenesis.org/kids/bugs/god-speaks-of-the- ant-in-his-word-the-bible/.

CHAPTER 8

1. Blue Letter Bible, s.v. "*ṭûḇ*," accessed July 10, 2023, https://www.blueletterbible.org/lexicon/h2898/kjv/ wlc/0-1/.

CHAPTER 9

1. Christine A. Lindberg, ed., *Oxford American Writer's Thesaurus, 3rd ed.* (New York: Oxford University Press, 2012), 80.
2. Blue Letter Bible, s.v. "*cheleb*," accessed July 10, 2023, https://www.blueletterbible.org/lexicon/ h2459/kjv/wlc/0-1/.